Hasinai

Hasinai

A TRADITIONAL HISTORY OF THE CADDO CONFEDERACY

Vynola Beaver Newkumet
and Howard L. Meredith

FOREWORD BY ARRELL MORGAN GIBSON

TEXAS A&M UNIVERSITY PRESS
COLLEGE STATION

First Edition

The paper used in this book meets the minimum requirements
of the American National Standard for Permanence
of Paper for Printed Library Materials, Z39.48-1984.
Binding materials have been chosen for durability.

Library of Congress Cataloging-in-Publication Data

Newkumet, Vynola Beaver, 1917–
Hasinai : a traditional history of the Caddo Confederacy / Vynola Beaver Newkumet and Howard L. Meredith ; foreword by Arrell Morgan Gibson. – 1st ed.
p. cm.
Bibliography: p.
Includes index.
ISBN 0-89096-342-8 (alk. paper) : $16.95
1. Caddo Indians–Dances. 2. Caddo Indians–Rites and ceremonies. 3. Indians of North America–Southwest, New–Dances. 4. Indians of North America–Southwest, New–Rites and ceremonies. I. Meredith, Howard L. II. Title.
E99.C12N48 1988
394'.3–dc19

88-16079
CIP

CONTENTS

ILLUSTRATIONS

FOREWORD

In the closing years of the twentieth century, Caddo peoples survive as a vital, functioning community in the American nation. Ancient life-directing talismans of fire and drum sustain these Native Americans with a potency no less than that of the eagle-and-freedom seal of their host.

This book relates the Caddo life epic, its origin and evolution before alien intrusion, its vicissitudes from confronting and reluctantly adjusting to a changing order, and its pained success in surviving to these times. Ethnic roots impart a persuasive credibility, a corroborative American Indian viewpoint, a ratifying element of folk history drawn from personal and collective experience.

The prehistoric and historical contexts of this story yield several instances of Caddo uniqueness, a dominating one that of continuing territorial residence. Most tribes under European and American dominion endured from one to several territorial relocations amounting to exiles. The Caddo occupied portions of their ancient homeland, albeit progressively diminished under successive imperial masters, throughout the alien imposition; even in the twentieth century they have resided on its western margins.

Hasinai presents archeological evidence of a rich pre-Columbian experience for Caddos as paleo-Indians, occupying a territory extending from Louisiana into eastern Texas and the lower margins of Arkansas and Oklahoma. A riverine-dwelling people, they concentrated their settlements in the Red River fertile alluvial bottomlands. Their lifestyle was advanced village sedentary. Caddos were preeminent farmers; men and women planted and cultivated fields of corn, their main crop, and beans, pumpkins, melons, squash, and tobacco. They were skilled in processing and storing the horticultural yield for the off-season and for commerce with plains-dwelling tribes. Caddos conducted annual trade fairs in their towns, drawing tribesmen from many parts.

Caddo men fashioned bows from bois d'arc and arrows from dogwood. They hunted buffalo, deer, elk, and other game for food and skins. Caddo women processed the furs and hides and from them fashioned clothing, household objects, and trade items. Before the European intrusion, Caddo craftsmen produced decorative utility and art objects from ceramic, shell, and wood materials.

On the eve of the European intrusion the Caddos numbered over eight thousand. Their primal sense of order led them to coalesce into political galaxies. Twenty-five Caddo settlements in Louisiana, Texas, Arkansas, and Oklahoma fused into three confederacies: the Hasinai, the largest, contained eight communities, situated primarily in eastern Texas; the Kadohadacho, four communities, located in the north along the Red River; and the Natchitoches, the smallest confederation, positioned downriver closest to the (later) French settlements in Louisiana.

The first aliens to reach the Caddos were Spaniards, members of Hernán de Soto's expedition, who arrived in this nation's lower river towns during the 1540s. Next came Frenchmen. Robert Cavalier, Sieur de La Salle, contacted Caddos during his explorations of the lower Mississippi valley during the late seventeenth century. This augured an extended relationship with the French. Much of the Caddo domain was situated in the territory La Salle designated as Louisiana, claimed by France.

Soon after 1700, French traders settled among the Caddos in their lower Red River towns. Experienced as wilderness merchants, Caddos became an important link in the French trade network, serving as middlemen for contacting more distant Indian tribes, carrying French goods to them and trafficking for their hides, furs, horses, mules, Spanish captives, and Indian slaves.

Shifting French and Spanish dominion over territories and peoples in the southwest brought periodic change to the Caddos. This book notes that both nations induced some economic and cultural change among these tribes, primarily in the adoption of and increasing dependence on European trade goods. Also both nations attempted some cultural alteration through assignment of Roman Catholic missionaries to the Caddos.

Mexican independence from Spain in 1821 brought little discernible change to Caddos in external relationships. Their most devastating changes came from the Anglo-American advent, first into Louisiana, Arkansas, and Texas after 1803, and into Texas after it was opened to settlement by non-Texans in 1819. Land-obsessed, agrarian-oriented "Long Knives" became the bane of Caddo territorial and demographic continuity. Disease and warfare, twin hells inflicted on the Caddos by the expansive intruders, produced an exponential decline in population and a concomitant malaise in tribal vitality and will to resist. As a result of these pressures, the Caddo removed themselves from their homelands in Louisiana, according to the Treaty of 1835, to Texas, then part of Mexico. A successful revolution in 1836 brought the Caddos back into direct conflict with the Anglo-Americans.

Caddos and other Indians suffered sustained torment from Anglo-American Texas during the era of the republic, and there was no respite after admission of Texas to the Union in 1845. The new state retained title to all public lands and federal officials found it nearly impossible to maintain a landed estate for resident tribes in face of the Texan expansionist juggernaut. Finally, in 1859, with the diminutive Brazos Reserve imperiled, federal agent Robert S. Neighbours collected the surviving Caddos and their ethnic cognates and, under military escort, led them over a "trail of tears" to southwestern Indian Territory and settled them on a reservation in the Leased District. As the disruptive, desolating imperial age for the Caddos came to a close, tribal elders commented that of all their alien masters they "preferred Frenchmen."

Beginning in 1901 under the terms of the General Allotment Act (Dawes Act), the Caddo reservation was partitioned and each enrolled Caddo was assigned an allotment of 160 acres and accorded United States citizenship. Federal law and policy were rigorously committed to eradicating all signs of Indianness in Native Americans under its jurisdiction. Federal rules enforced on reservations by government agents included banning tribal religion, dress, art, marriage, and family practices, government, and every other ethnic manifestation. Resisting Indians were punished. The national goal was to americanize, to transform every Indian into a hybrid Anglo-American. Agents applied this cultural erasure process to the Caddos.

However, as this work shows, the ancient, esteemed cultural roots worked deep in the natures of the Hasinai. Environmental and cosmic sources nourished them in this new travail and encouraged them to persevere in the old ways. The drum, fire, and dance rituals, observed clandestinely, maintained their resolve. Finally, their cultural suppression ended during the 1930s with passage of the Indian Reorganization Act and the Oklahoma Indian Welfare Act. Cherished Caddo ways could again be observed openly.

This book exults in the Caddo deliverance. The drum, fire, dances, and recitation of the epic songs confirm the continuity of Caddo culture and polity. In the Caddo universe tribal members once again may meditate and pursue the seemingly impossible, which they aver forces them "beyond the borders of ordinary discourse."

ARRELL MORGAN GIBSON
George Lynn Cross Research Professor of History
Department of History
University of Oklahoma
Norman, Oklahoma

PREFACE

Although it is impossible to do justice to the Hasinai experience within the narrow confines of one volume, it has become increasingly important to attempt syntheses of our perspectives. Pursuit of the impossible, after all, pushes us beyond the borders of ordinary discourse. Throughout the history of the Hasinai, understanding of its heritage has passed from generation to generation through the family and ceremonial experiences. It will continue to do so, even though the Hasinai live great distances from one another and the secular world intervenes more and more.

A people needs to examine, every so often, the framework of understanding within which scholarship and ordinary daily life are conducted. Trying to strike a balance between subjective experience and objective observation, Vynola B. Newkumet and I attempted to compile a synthesis of the Hasinai lifestyle. Trying to view the whole of the Hasinai past through the narrowing prism needed for a one-volume work, we were forced to concentrate on the really major landmarks. We studied the traditions that underlay the historical landscape. Even if our understandings—personal and historical—did not always dovetail, they may provide for others a view of the heritage of the American southwest.

The framework for most studies of human life in the past several centuries has been divided into "prehistory" and "history," writing being the basis for division. We recalled the familiar progressions from Stone Age to Bronze Age to Iron Age and from ancient to medieval to modern. These are strangely discordant terms to apply to the Hasinai past.

The traditions of affiliate communities of the Hasinai show continuity in terms of customs, standards, beliefs, and relative geographic proximity. These communities include the Haish, Hainai, Yona, Kechai, Nadaco, Nasoni, Kadohadacho, as well as the Natchitoche. Symbols and images are handed on and modified as they have been for centuries. Traditional values become the measure of conduct by defining its purposes and even its means. They are the focus of this work.

West European rational, empirical knowledge has weakened confidence in the accumulated wisdom of practical experience. Tasks have been created and taken up in this century that seem to be far too complex to be dealt with by recourse to traditional forms of knowledge. The traditional Hasinai ways of conceiving of the world and of human life would seem to be out of place. Western rational thought, stemming from Greek intellectual norms, is in command throughout most of North America.

But appearances can be deceptive. The Hasinai live and work in their own way. Rational West European patterns of thought have been taught to virtually everyone. Thus reason *and* tradition are in place for problem-solving. Hasinai tradition sums up a mass of historical experience rooted in centuries of life in the American southwest.

Apparent conflicts between reason and tradition make it increasingly difficult to maintain a sense of balance in contemporary affairs. Human beings need the aid of past generations. Civilization is based upon collective responses preserved in a given region. Loss of contact with the accomplishments of ancestors is injurious to later generations because it deprives them of guidance. West European societies have taken too much to heart the command to innovate, to always look for new ways, as if this were the only goal to be pursued.

Oral tradition forms the main source for this book. Materials have been collected in both Hasinai and English. The use of phonetic spelling as they heard it for Hasinai words, showing accented syllables, was decided upon by Phil and Vynola Newkumet at the beginning of the collecting period. Rather than adopting standard pronunciation symbols which would not be familiar to the general reader, they decided to keep the system as simple as possible, for the future use of Caddo young people in Oklahoma. The notations served this function. Vynola and Phil kept separate lists of words throughout the years. When this volume was written, these lists were compared and a single phonetic spelling selected as being easiest for the nonspecialist to use.

Published and manuscript English, Spanish, and French materials primarily represent government and church agencies—exogenous sources. Oral sources are the most legitimate representations of Hasinai traditions, which do not lend themselves easily to Anglo-American categories. Rather, the history of the Hasinai is distilled to its most refined state in the drum dance and the turkey dance. The Hasinai of the Southwest performed their ceremonials for centuries before the arrival of the Europeans. These dances provided a needed ritual structure for their life together. Vynola and I felt that a description of these dances would serve as the best and most "authentic" framework for this volume.

The ceremonials now take place at the Caddo Tribal Complex near Binger, Oklahoma, every month during the summer. In the afternoon, the turkey dance is done by the women to interpret the historical events still significant to the Hasinai. In the evenings the drum dance takes each participant through the very same emergence sequence that every Hasinai tribal member has relived for thousands of years. Then the dances continue through the night, each in its turn. The ceremonials last from two to four days and nights, and the two longest come in the late summer. One is conducted in association with the American Indian Exposition in August, which is held in nearby Anadarko, Oklahoma. The other is held over the Labor Day weekend in September. Hasinai ceremonial life is bound up in traditional songs and dances—sacred reflections of what it means to be Hasinai. Each ceremonial is a pivotal expression of the people in community. All of these rites express the joy that results from the community of the people within the spiritual context. Where there is joy there is no fear. The tendency of some people who live near the Caddo in contemporary Oklahoma has been to dismiss as romantic or sentimental the efforts to continue traditional tribal expression in dance and song. However, the comprehensive support of these cultural expressions of being and the scholarly examination of them are of central importance to our cultural future.

Vynola Beaver Newkumet and I spent several years of work on this volume. We traveled across the traditional Hasinai homeland in July, 1982, seeking out sites around Natchitoches and Caddo Lake in Louisiana, Nacogdoches in Texas, and the Red River and Washita valleys in Oklahoma. She went to her last dance at the Caddo Tribal Complex north of Anadarko in September and then went home to Norman, Oklahoma, where she died later that year.

Acknowledgment, with appreciation, is made to Phil Newkumet, Irving Whitebead, Arrell M. Gibson, and Reathia Cussen for reading the manuscript in its entirety and offering important commentary. I alone am responsible for the final drafts, although I have tried to remain true to the thoughts and feelings Vynola expressed during our work together.

–HOWARD L. MEREDITH

Hasinai

ONE

Drum Dance

ORIGINS

The *cah-kit-em'-bin* or drum dance is always the initial dance of the night's cycle of dances for the Hasinai people. The dance retells the story of Hasinai origins. The men lead, carrying the drum. Some of these leaders are singers and some are drummers. They circle the dance ground, moving clockwise, in harmony with the earth's movement. Initially, there was a sequence of eleven songs, relating the origins and early heritage of the Hasinai. Irving Whitebead is one of the few singers left who know all the songs. He sat and sang with his father so that he could learn them all. In these songs, specific events are related about the Hasinai transition from the preceding world into the southwest, where they have lived now for centuries. Young boys are allowed to join the lead singers, so that they may become familiar with the songs, but they are not allowed to beat the drum. As the dance proceeds around the dance ground, other men and women join the singers and drummers, following their lead.

The second segment of the *cah-kit-em'-bin,* known as the *wah-sha-nee'-kee,* begins after a short pause. In this portion, the drummers are in the middle of the dance ground. The pace is faster than in the first segment. The drummers rotate in the center of the dance area; the dancers continue to move in the direction of the earth around the center. The *cah-kit-em'-bin* usually lasts about one hour. The Hasinai have moved through their history each time the dance is performed. It makes them one with their ancestors.

At the heart of Hasinai existence are the cultural traditions that carry the people through space and time.[1] In the movement of dance and the language of song, the reality of existence is projected into the future. This experience is closely linked to the region in which they still live. The Hasinai have lived for centuries in the region now known as the American southwest. This homeland encompasses much of the present states of Arkansas, Louisiana, Oklahoma, and Texas. Hasinai traditions have been shaped by centuries of life in the region. The Hasinai live in accord with their environment as few others can. Their power comes in part from their homeland.

The songs of the *cah-kit-em'-bin* tell of the beginning in which the heavens and earth were very different from their present form. In the earliest times, darkness ruled over the land. In this darkness only one man lived as a Hasinai. Around him, a village emerged. As its occupants grew in number, they noticed that the man seemed to be everywhere. Then he disappeared, only to return with all types of food in the form of seeds. The unknown man called the people together and patiently explained that the seeds were food for Hasinai use. He then gave the seeds to each of the people who were present.

The man also told the people that the darkness would not rule all the time, as it had in the past. The Hasinai would see, with a new sense of vision, all that was in existence around them. They were given the pledge that a new being would be with them, whose name would be *sah-cooh,* the sun. This new being was to be given tremendous power by Ah-ah-ha'-yo, the "Father Above." When the place and time would come for *sah-cooh*'s appearance, he would be called out from his mother. The people were told also that the direction from which *sah-cooh* would come would be known as the east. The direction in which it would disappear from view would be known as the west. *Sah-cooh* was the first entity created by Ah-ah-ha'-yo. The Hasinai would see the sun as never before in their existence.

The unknown man indicated that the people, in its new existence, should have a leader. This man should be called *cah-de,* "chief." The *cah-de* should be the wisest and most able among them. He should be obeyed in all things and should be looked upon as a "great father." The man, who still remained unknown, told the Hasinai to return to their homes and hold council among themselves to select a *cah-de*.

When they went into council, a man by the name of Ta'-sha (wolf), told the people that the powerful unknown man should be called Neesh (moon). This was because he was the first among the Hasinai. After careful consideration, the man called Neesh was decided upon as the *cah-de*. Finally, Neesh called the Hasinai together again. He asked them if they had made their choice. Ta'-sha reported that they had decided upon him and that he should be known by the name Neesh. He agreed to accept this leadership position and then selected an aide. Ta'-sha was selected to call the people together for council. He was to be known as the *tum-mah*, or village crier.

On one memorable occasion, the *tum'-mah* was sent out to tell the Hasinai that the *cah-de* wanted them to assemble. Neesh had very important news to tell them. They should gather as quickly as possible. When they had assembled, the *cah-de* sent the *tum'-mah* around to all of them with instructions that they be divided into groups, because there were so many of them. Further, each group should have a leader, who would be given a drum. The people formed itself into groups and selected a leader, known as a *cah-nah-ha* or community head man, for each group. The *cah-de* called these leaders together and gave each one a drum. He explained to the *cah-nah-ha* that they must sing and beat their drums as the people moved from the world in darkness to the new world. Furthermore, none of them were to look back behind them. If they stopped on the way, they would have to stay there in the dark.

Upon the signal from the *cah-de* the people began moving to the west, emerging in groups in a new world of light. While groups were still coming out into the light, Ta'-sha came out with his group. In the new world he observed a figure with horns and a tail. He decided to stop and warn the others who were following. Ta'-sha spoke to warn the others. All of the people who had not emerged stopped and were trapped. They were left in the world of darkness.

The place where the people emerged into the new world became known as *Cha-cah-nee-nah* or "place of crying." The exact location is not known. It has been identified by some as the mouth of a cave in the side of a hill on the south bank of the *Bah'-hat-te-no* or Red River, at its junction with the *Bah'-ha Sah-sin* or Mississippi River. Others indicate the place of origin at the edge of Sodo Lake, also in what is now Louisiana. The people who had arrived in the new world sat down and cried over the loss of those who were left in the old world. This gave the place its name, *Cha-cah-nee-nah.* Because the Hasinai emerged from the earth, they call it *E'-nah-wah'-dut;* literally, "mother dirt."

When the first people emerged into the new world, the men, aside from the leaders, carried pipes and pieces of flint. The women carried the seed corn and pumpkin seeds that had been given to them in the old world. Each of these material things is very important to the Hasinai. They have always attempted to hold fast to these things. Although there were periods of difficulty, when some of these things would be lost, the Hasinai have never thrown them away.

The appearances of the new world in the light were beautiful. As the ice sheets and snow receded to the north, a cooler climate prevailed than is normal now. In time the seasons began to approach what is now considered normal. A mild, windy spring with light, frequent showers preceded a moderately moist summer that was hot by day and warm by night. This was followed by a dry, cool, prolonged fall and a winter that was short, but with occasional spells of severe weather.

The soils to the north and west of the *Bah'-hat-te-no* in the lands that became the extended homeland of the Hasinai are primarily pedalfers. By far, the largest part of the region is covered by red and yellow soils. Red soils cover the areas of good drainage where the water table lies many feet below the surface, whereas yellow soils lie in flat areas where ground water comes near the surface. These are all forest soils. They are predominantly sandy in the surface horizons.

The people created the majority of the ceremonial centers and villages in the river valleys. The dominant soils along their courses are alluvial in origin, rich in organic materials, and usually dark in color. The organic materials are washed downstream from the Great Plains. Corn and pumpkin were grown in almost every type of soil in the region; the greatest yields came from the darkest colored soils. The most important valleys besides the *Bah'-hat-te-no* or Red River were the *Cooh'-cooh-ah-tsi-yo* or Sabine River, the *Cah-ye-tsi* or Neches River, and the *Nah-cha-wi* or Angelina River.

This homeland is a timbered region dominated by pines – longleaf, loblolly, shortleaf, and slash. In the valleys, hardwoods such as pecan, hickory, and walnut were mixed with the pines; gum, oak, and cypress were also to be found. Of the many varieties of trees that flourish in the region, the hardwoods – bois d'arc and dogwood – were extremely important to the Hasinai. The bois d'arc or osage orange wood is heavy, exceedingly hard, strong, and durable. The heartwood has a bright orange color, turning brown upon exposure. It was used to make the finest bows, for both private use and trade. The Hasinai bows were sought throughout the southwest, as far as the Rio Grande valley. The wood was also a source of dye to make materials a light brown color. The dogwood shoots made excellent arrows. The wood was workable, so that arrows could be made straight and true.

The first important center of Hasinai activities in the new world was called "Tall-timber-on-top-of-the-hill," near what is now Caddo Lake on the present border of Louisiana and Texas. It was near there that Neesh called the Hasinai together for the first time after they had entered the region of light. He told them that Ah-ah-ha'-yo had sent a child to them. The child would grow and teach the people right from wrong. It was also told that the child would name himself Cah-e-sti.

A man and his wife in the principal village had four daughters. Each was beautiful and well behaved. As they grew into young women, part of their tasks was to gather *e'-ha-si-nai,* wild potatoes. Each time they went to the low places where the *e'-ha-si-nai* grew, three of the young women were successful and one never found any. After many failures, the young woman wandered slowly through the area, when she heard a cry, "Mother." She looked around, but could find no one. Again she heard the voice coming to her and then she knew it was in her womb. A little boy had come to help her. The voice told her to go to a specific place. She followed the instructions and found many large *e'-ha-si-nai.* In four months' time, the young woman showed she was pregnant. In ten months, the little boy was born.

The mother and child lived apart from the others. They were poor and hungry much of the time, for they had no one to hunt for them. All they had to eat was what others gave them. The child grew rapidly and had many adventures in his youth. He named himself Cah-e-sti. Others have recorded that his name was Ha-coo-shoo Cah-e-sti. He was directed by Ah-ah-ha'-yo to distinguish what was valued as good from what was harmful.

During this same period, there was a rough fellow who went down to the water, where the four sisters went. He was an orphan who lived alone with his grandmother. He became an excellent hunter also. At one time, he had a splinter in his knee. It became infected. In time a child came of this infection. The hunter would have nothing to do with the child, but the grandmother cared for it. The boy grew to manhood in the same period as Cah-e-sti. In fact, they killed a water monster together. But in time, the boy became wary of the persons around him. He felt they would kill him, if they had the opportunity. He found the power to bewitch the people. Only Cah-e-sti finally stopped him from his evil activities. Between the behavior of the two, the people could easily see the choice of *ha'-ah-hut* or good and *ha-ba-la* or bad.

Cah-e-sti also introduced the use of bows and arrows to the Hasinai. He spoke to the people about bows and arrows, telling of their use in hunting. He also indicated that they should be used by men only. In the earliest period, hunting had been no problem, but in time it became more difficult. The people at first used large lances and later threw darts to bring down game for food. The bow and arrow made hunting more effective once again.

Originally, not only hunting was easy, but crops were no difficulty. Every community practiced farming. This was not wholly from necessity, but it added to the diet beyond the foods the people collected. The Hasinai were productive. Rarely did they resort to raiding others for their wealth.

Many villages appeared in those first generations, varying in size from fifty to two hundred inhabitants. Around each village were clearings for agriculture. It is said that clearing was done first by burning the undergrowth and then killing the larger trees by making incisions into the sapwood. This caused the trees to die gradually. As sunlight penetrated through the withering branches, planting began. Each community planted seeds in small hills dug with sticks and hoes of bone and flint. Plant and animal matter were used as fertilizer. Initially, corn and pumpkin were the primary crops, but beans and squash were added to the people's wealth. All of these were often planted intermixed in the same field or even in the same small hill. The stumps of the larger trees would usually remain throughout the life of the clearing being used as a planting field.

A diminishing yield in a field after several years normally led to the clearing of new fields within easy reach of the villages. It was observed also that both grass and shrubby undergrowth advanced rapidly in burnt-over tracts. This protected the villages from chance fires of natural origin. There was always considerable restraint in the use of fire, because the advantage of cleared fields was obtained at the heavy price of the destruction of fruits and berries.

It was told that in time, the Hasinai noticed that their *cah-de,* Neesh, paid no attention to them. He seemed to have nothing to say. He did not call them together anymore, but stayed at his home all the time. The people began to think that there must be something wrong. Neesh was setting a bad example for his people. Young Cah-e-sti knew all about this, for he had a greater sense of power than did Neesh.

Living in the center of the village with his parents, Neesh had never married. Unknown to his father and mother, he had been going at night to force himself upon his sister, who was younger than he. She did not know who he was in the dark. One night she decided to mark him. She put some black paint on her fingers. She marked him across his forehead in such a way that he would not know what she had done. In the morning, Neesh came before her. She saw the marks on his forehead. She knew her brother had forced himself upon her. His sister could not live like this and so she told others. When Neesh learned that his wrongdoing was becoming common knowledge, he became so ashamed that he wished to leave his people. Soon he passed away, called by Ah-ah-ha'-yo. To this day, the Hasinai are reminded of Neesh as he is symbolized in the night sky by the face of the moon, where all the people can see him and the shame marks across his forehead.

The Hasinai came together to select another *cah-de*. Young Cah-e-sti was the choice of the people. His first pronouncement was that the Hasinai must move farther west. This was done with some difficulty. In the people's travels, there was growing alienation between the Hasinai and the animals. Hunting became more difficult. The men had to travel long distances to take game with their bows and arrows.

Even after the Hasinai began to hunt the animals, they remained on friendly terms with many of them. All of the animals had a wonderful sense of power. They sometimes appeared to the people in dreams. That vision of power was used in turn to aid others. Often when men were out hunting and were left alone in the forest at night, the animals came to them and related their sense of power. This then worked through the hunter to the benefit of all the people.

After a man had a dream of power, he went home, where he remained in silence for several days. During this time, he meditated upon what was revealed to him. At the end of this period, he asked the elders and his friends to his home, where he related the essence of the dream. If the men wished it, he then taught them the vision of power in song and dance.

The first men to receive this type of vision of power and give a dance were two young brothers. They were hunters. Nightfall came upon them before they could return to camp. So they slept in the woods, because they were very tired. In their sleep, they both had a dream in which they met each other and then traveled to the east. On their way, they saw a man traveling toward them at a rapid pace moving toward the west. They met him and conversed with him in Hasinai. After a long conversation, the man took a bag that he carried and told them to choose any kind of medicine they wished. But he handed them one, saying that if they wished to live long and be difficult to kill, they should take this one. When the two brothers accepted the medicine, the man took a long time to explain how to use it. Then he left them, taking up his trip to the west. At dawn, both of the brothers woke up and each one remembered the dream, but said nothing to the other. They traveled home again. After several months, they each began to try the medicine.

Two years later, conflict was renewed with the warlike Chickasaw people. They traveled into the Hasinai country to kill and take prisoners. The Chickasaw were victorious in this attack on the Hasinai. They left death and destruction to return again across the *Bah'-ha Sah-sin.* Every night when they made camp, the Chickasaw danced around their prisoners, who were bound and placed in the center of the great "ring of dancers." Each night after the dancing was over, the prisoners lay cold and exhausted. However, one of them was able to escape. It was nearly dawn. He had not gone very far when he heard the Chickasaws coming after him. He did not know what do to. About to give up, he noticed a hollow log and slipped inside it. The Chickasaws failed to find him. Only after it was dark again, he crawled out of the log and started home. After two days, he reached the village and told his story.

There were many men who had been away on a hunt during the attack by the Chickasaw war band. Among those who had returned to the village were the two brothers. By this time, the Chickasaws were about five days on their trek back to their homeland. But the Hasinai men started after them. The elder of the two brothers, Strong Wind, was chosen to lead the retaliatory party. After several days, they came upon the overconfident Chickasaw war party. The Hasinai discovered the camp at night. They could hear the drums and victory songs. The night was very dark, so it was decided to wait until dawn to make the attack. At the first light, the Hasinai rushed into the camp and killed many of the Chickasaw. Strong Wind and his brother fought with the power of ten men. They rushed into the midst of the enemy. The Chickasaws were powerless against them. Even the Hasinai stopped fighting to stare in wonder at the bravery of the two brothers. The few Chickasaw who were left fled away to the east in terror. The Hasinai collected those who had been captives. They returned to their home with joy in their hearts.

For many years, the brothers practiced medicine to heal the sick. They also fought with valor to help preserve the Hasinai homeland. A society of medicine men grew up around their vision of power. In time, two types of medicine came to be differentiated. First there was the kind that had power to heal the sick and infirm. A second type had the power to prevent someone from being hurt or harmed. As life became more difficult, medicine grew in importance.

A time of difficulty followed this period, when the Hasinai lost the drum and all it symbolized. Some say it was taken from them by a devil, *tsa-kee'-yooh.* There was a tremendous disruption in the life of the Hasinai. After an interminable period, a man came to where four Hasinai were sitting under a *sah'-ah* or box elder tree. He placed a bundle in a fork of the *sah'-ah* and then left. Lightning struck the tree and the drum came out of the bundle. The Hasinai men took it, so that the people regained the drum. Even today, the Hasinai have both flint and coal inside their drums. Fire was essential to life. The drum and the fire are linked inextricably in the life of the Hasinai. This comes from this early reclamation of the drum. Lightning and thunder are one, symbolized by the flint in the drum.

The origins and collective thought of the Hasinai are reflected in the drum dance cycle. This tradition is complex; it frees the individual within society to reflect on the vision that is singularly for that person. It is not a mere straitjacket of conventions. Hasinai tradition awakens a sense of independence. Only when persons have reflected on their particular vision of the cosmos are they free to enter society. Only then will each person be able to contribute to it in a correct way. Civilization cannot exist without knowledge of ancestors. In the same way, there is no civilization without freedom of choice on the part of the individual. These thoughts are the critical foundation of the material and spiritual culture of Hasinai civilization.

TWO

Bear Dance

HUNTING

Those who sing with the drum are seated at the west edge of the dance arena. As the first song starts, those who want to join in the dance come into the arena in pairs, women usually on the left and men on the right in each pair. Pairs move around slowly in a wide counterclockwise circle. One couple dances behind the other. They start, facing straight ahead, with a change to half-facing each other at a cue from the singers—a few accentuated higher notes and drum beats. These changes come about a minute or less apart, alternating from straight ahead to half-facing each other, with short left-right steps. The last four or five songs are more lively and rapid. The dancing changes pattern, as each one of a pair dance, first face to face, men dancing forward, women backward, then changing at the cue by turning as a pair so that the woman now moves forward, the man backward. In all of the dances where persons are lined up one behind another, everyone should be in step.

Over the centuries, the physical and technological aspects of obtaining meat to sustain life among the Hasinai have changed tremendously. Only one aspect has remained constant. That is prayer. Every morning the Hasinai men, whether they were hunters, ranchers, or draftsmen, rise to offer prayers of thanksgiving to Ah-ah-ha'-yo. They understand that the creative spirit that guides the universe provides for them. The men's expressed appreciation is the principal thing they can return for the gifts that sustain life.

The physical changes in the environment over the centuries necessitated corresponding changes in the means of providing animal foods. The entire range of the Hasinai homeland is found within the western extension of the Gulf Coastal Plain, in what is now Arkansas, Louisiana, Oklahoma, and Texas. Analysis of animal remains of the region dominated by the Hasinai has indicated major changes in the environment in the past. The animal evidence associated with freshwater ponds unearthed in several locations in the region indicate a great change several thousand years ago during the last glacial recession. The nature of the environment in the region was influenced by the surface layer of meltwater that covered much of the Gulf of Mexico. This brought to an end a cycle of relative aridity that had prevailed through much of the last glacial period. The dry climate was the result of the reduced frequency of tropical storms because of a lower ocean temperature. It is theorized that the Gulf Stream may have followed a southerly course toward the Iberian Peninsula rather than toward the British Isles. The equatorial oceans were as much as 6 degrees centigrade lower in surface temperature. The sea level was at least eighty-five meters lower than its present measure. Midsummer temperatures on the land of the region of the Hasinai were as much as 15 degrees centigrade lower than present averages. Core studies indicate that vegetation changed noticeably around forty-seven hundred years ago.[1]

With the changes in the environment came different animal populations. Earlier sources of food were lost, the large game animals – the mammoth, the mastodon, the giant buffalo, among others. In time, the principal sources of meat and hides became the deer and the bear. Even later the buffalo became increasingly important. By the late nineteenth and early twentieth century, there was limited hunting of bear in the Wichita Mountains and deer on the plains to the west. But beef cattle largely replaced the other sources of meat. The Hasinai word for meat is *cah-oo'-tooh;* the word for beef is *wah-cus cah-oo'-tooh.*

Hunting tales reflect the importance that this skill once represented. Hunting was never a full-time occupation. The men would leave their homes for days at a time. They hunted in the forests or the plains, or went fishing on the rivers. These expeditions were done in cooperation with others. The hunting group was a disciplined organization, with leadership gained through ability. Hunting dogs were used for specific game animals. Some dogs were deer dogs; others were trained to hunt bear. The variety of game hunted in the past was large. In the forest, there was deer, peccary, and bear. There were also many birds, the most important of which were wild turkeys. On the plains were antelope and buffalo. In ponds and marshes were ducks of various kinds. In the rivers were fish and turtles of many sorts. In the spring of each year, the men would travel to the Gulf Coast to hunt and fish.

In the past, bows and arrows were used exclusively. Rifles, introduced by European traders, later replaced them. Arrows were tipped with a variety of substances, including flint, bone, shell, and metal. Dogwood shafts were hardened with fire at the tip. Much of the men's success in killing birds and game was due to their wonderful skill in imitating natural cries. The Hasinai knew how to hunt best in the valleys of the Red, Angelina, and the Neches rivers. After removal to the upper Brazos Reserve and later to Indian Territory, hunting was much more difficult, for the strange country made it very difficult.

In these new areas, the Texas and then the federal government took responsibility for supplying the Hasinai and other Caddo tribes with meat. Usually it was beef. The preparation of the beef was little different from the centuries-old processes for preparation of other types of meat. The steer was slaughtered near the home. The meat was cut into thin strips about six to eight inches in length. These were sun dried. Some of the strips were put into an oven and roasted, then dried in the house. Some of the dried *wah-cus cah-oo'-tooh* was placed in the *ki'-cooh,* walnut mortar and pestle. The beef was then pounded into fine fibers, with the fat being pulverized along with the lean. All the different types of preserved beef were packed into sacks and stored in an outbuilding constructed for that express purpose. Usually one steer was slaughtered for a single family each year. Like the bear and the deer, all parts of the animal were used for some purpose.

The intestine of the steer was boiled and turned inside out. Usually it was then filled with dried meat or sometimes with fresh meat. The stomach was boiled and eaten at the time of the slaughter. Its consistency was that of gristle. The tongue was boiled and eaten at the same time. The brains were used for tanning the hide.

In most instances, a family had three or four hides of different types in the tanning process at any one time.[2]

The principal difference between the preparation of bear meat and beef was the rendering of the grease. The bear oil was useful in a number of ways. It was good to cook in and to burn in a lamp. Perfumed bear oil in small amounts kept the hair in beautiful shape.

First steps in the tanning process were taken during the slaughter. The first thing was to stretch the hide tight, with the raw side up. All the remaining skin was removed. If making buckskin or rawhide, it was then taken down and soaked in an ash solution to help remove the hair. The brains of the beef or buffalo were taken and boiled in water; then the solution was strained. This fine brain solution was used in tanning the skin. Again it was hung out to dry. After it was softened by drying, it was taken and smoked, if desired. This gave a darker finish. The Hasinai never used raw skin. When a skin became soiled, it could be cleaned by scrubbing with fine, dried white clay or cornmeal.

Fresh game was hunted and prepared throughout the year. This included deer, rabbit, and squirrel, even into the twentieth century. Wild fowl, particularly turkey, prairie chicken, and quail, as well as geese and ducks, continued to be important to the diet. The turkey and the Hasinai have lived in close proximity for centuries. Originally, Hasinai villages were established in close proximity to large turkey roosts. The turkey is still considered in closer association to the people than is any other animal. The wild turkeys were important not only as a source of food, but as a source of feathers and for protection as well. After agricultural development expanded as a basis for society, turkeys were drawn to the villages because of the abundance of corn available to them. Flocks roosted at the edge of the village settlements. They provided warning against night travelers when they approached the outskirts of population centers.

Villages were always located near fresh running water, and hence fishing was an important means of supplementing the diet. The most practical means of catching fish, which continued to be used into the twentieth century, was the trotline, which was secured at both ends so that it crossed the water course. Hooks were attached

Inkinash family killing beef, Anadarko, Oklahoma, around 1879. BELOW: Caddo ranchers.

Caddo village. *Courtesy Soule Collection, Western History Collections, University of Oklahoma Library*

Thomas Wister, called Mr. Blue, and Stanley Edge, a Caddo. *Phillips Collection, Western History Collections, University of Oklahoma Library*

Yummit, Nora Dunlap, and Mary Hunter. *Phillips Collection, Western History Collections, University of Oklahoma Library*

Peter Williams.

Harris Conner and James Hunter.

Alice Williams (left) and Margaret Sargent.

Willie Weller (Ti-Yun), Minco ball player, 1908.

Vynola Newkumet at tribal dance, 1938. *Courtesy Oklahoma Historical Society*

Caddo delegates to Shreveport Centennial, 1935. BELOW: Caddo family, 1938.

Caddo delegation to Shreveport Centennial, June 28–July 1, 1935. From left: Ralph Murrow, Charles Parton Smith, Mrs. Charles P. Smith, Mrs. Ben Carter, Joe Johnson, Ben Carter, Alice Cussen, Mrs. Charles Adams, Melva Jean Murrow, Charles Adams (chief), ______ Smith, Helen Murrow, Josephine Inkanish, Harry Edge (2nd chief), Mrs. Harry Edge, Mrs. Fritz Hendrix, Mrs. Alfred Taylor, Alfred Taylor, Thomas Merle Keyes, Jr., LeRoy Johnson, Mrs. Ralph Murrow, Thomas Keyes, Sr., C. Ross Hume, Fritz Hendrix, Stanley Edge. Mrs. Thomas Keyes was not pictured.

about a step apart. The trotlines were set and the fish taken from the hooks, which were then baited again with worms or dough. In addition, freshwater clams were collected along the sand banks where a river curved in its course. The clams were also a source of pearls, of the same type found by the thousands in Craig Mound at the Spiro Mound Complex on the Arkansas River.

Hunting was never as important to the Hasinai in Oklahoma as it had been in eastern Texas and northwestern Louisiana. Skills acquired over the centuries were not transferable to the new country. During the second half of the nineteenth century, bear could still be hunted in the Wichita Mountains and buffalo on the Great Plains. But the freedom of the hunt was curtailed by the armed forces of the United States government and by the mass slaughter of animals on the Great Plains by pioneers and developers. Government-issued beef became a mainstay. Yet small animals were still in great supply until the beginning of the twentieth century when Indian Territory was cannibalized by federal politicians to create the state of Oklahoma. Hasinai interests had been turning to the west for several hundred years prior to their removal in the nineteenth century. They still knew how and where to hunt and fish as long as the boomer spirit did not destroy the game. New priorities did not allow for the use of refined skills required in the past.

THREE

Corn Dance

AGRICULTURE

This popular social dance is started when the singers and the drum come toward the center of the arena with the beginning song of the corn dance, *kish-sih'-cah-oh'-shun.* The dancers fall in behind the drum, in side-by-side pairs, all women usually on the left at the beginning of the dance, each person half-facing his or her partner. As more join the dance, a large circle is formed moving counterclockwise, in a lively near-side step, left foot in step with partner's right foot, right foot with partner's left foot. At each cue from the singers and drum, each one changes place with the partner, all women then being on the right, alternating each time. At the end of each song there is a pause, with the usual crossover change of places. Usually there is also some whooping and hollering by the singers and answering in kind by some of the dancers.

The Hasinai appreciate the earth and revere it. Without its support, the people could not exist. In the twentieth century, the men were up at dawn and out into the fields, just as had been the tradition for families through the centuries. Prayer began each new day. These prayers were ones of thanksgiving and appreciation. The men walked the rows of crops and studied the plants. It was important to observe and understand the crops, the wild plants, and trees in their response to the weather. Their adaptations to the changing seasons and environment were critical to understanding their rhythm of growth. Observations of this sort were major topics of discussion in the home—the budding of the trees or the growth of the corn and beans. A feeling of love permeated all these talks.[1]

Love of and respect for the land and growing things were passed

down from one generation to the next in the everyday experience of the Hasinai. This was their tradition, centered on settled agriculture and domestic animals. That tradition and its survival have been respected throughout the existence of the people. The uprootedness of the current age has made this style of life increasingly more difficult. Yet even with modern adaptations, this tradition is still a guarantor of order and of civilization despite the chaos that surrounds it.

From the time of the emergence of the Hasinai from the earth, respect has been given *e'-nah-wah'-dut* as a mother. In that beginning the Hasinai received gifts that they were to hold and use for their benefit. The two gifts most closely associated with the earth were *kish-sih'*, corn, and *coo-nooh-cah-ke-cus'-neh*, pumpkin.

Of the two gifts, *kish-sih'* has come into the greatest use and respect. The people planted the *kish-sih'* as soon as the last threat of frost had ended for the spring. The ground had been cleared from the previous plantings the preceding fall. After planting, there was one pass through the fields to weed, while the corn was still small. At the time when the corn was about to ripen, usually in late July in Oklahoma, it was watched very carefully.

At the appropriate time, the men dug trenches that were rectangular in shape, with slanting sides. Angles at the bottom of the trench were all greater than ninety degrees. The trench was always about as deep as an ear-and-a-half of corn. Wood was brought in and piled by the trenches to supply the fire keeper. It was his responsibility to keep the heat regulated at the proper intensity. A new fire could not be started. The process began before the corn was brought in from the fields.

When the corn was ripe, the men gathered and moved to the fields in wagons and trucks. In the twentieth century, this always included the men of several related families. The corn was gathered as quickly as possible, filling wagon after wagon. The corn was allowed to sit one night before anyone began to process it. By this time, the fire was started and kept under control.

The morning after it was harvested, everyone, regardless of age, began shucking the corn. A large portion of the crop was shucked by merely pulling back the outside covering from the ear. This allowed easier handling. The fire was brought to the right level in the trench. Then the corn was placed along the sides of the trench. The shucks showed above the surface of the ground. It was the duty of the young children to turn the corn in the trench so that it was roasted evenly.

When the corn was roasted, it was pulled out of the trench and placed on a spread canvas. There it was allowed to cool. When it could be handled, the ears were shelled, using only one's hands. The kernels came off the cob easily. They were collected in sacks for storage. The sacks were hung up in the barn and the storehouse to be brought out as needed through the year.

Some of the parched corn was processed into *kish-wah'*. The corn was pounded into a fine powder in the *ki'-cooh,* a large mortar and pestle made out of hard wood, often black walnut. The powder was taken from the *ki'-cooh* when the hollow began to fill. This powder was strained through a round screening pan. When shaken, the fine corn fell through the strainer and landed on a large towel. The rougher material went back into the *ki'-cooh.* The *kish-wah'* could be eaten in its powdered form or with honey or sugar. It was also formed into patties by adding water to it. This was known as *kin-neh'*. Both *kish-wa'* and *kin-neh'* could be used alone or boiled with dried meat. It became a thickening agent for stew or soup. Both forms were stored away for food preparation throughout the year.

While corn was being parched at harvest time, another means of preservation was being carried out by the women. This was the preparation of *dush'-cut-duc-ka'*. Fresh corn was scraped from the cob. Women in recent times use lids from cans perforated to make a grater. The kernels, when scraped from the cob, left a mushy corn substance in the pans where it was collected. A little shortening or bacon grease was added to the corn at this stage. Then the mixture was baked in a medium oven for about one-half to three-quarters of an hour. When it was browned, the corn was taken out to cool. While it was still warm, the *dush'-cut-duc-ka'* was broken into small pieces. This was then taken out to dry.

The pieces were placed on a large piece of canvas, which was taken up to a low pitched roof of a small building or an arbor. The pieces were turned in the morning and the afternoon by the children. The entire canvas was folded over on the *dush'-cut-duc-ka'* at dusk. The procedure was repeated beginning the next morning at dawn, when the canvas was reopened and the corn spread over its surface again. This process was repeated for about five days. When the *dush'-cut-duc-ka'* was completely dry, it was stored in sacks. These also were hung in the storage house. To prepare the *dush'-cut-duc-ka'* for a meal, several servings were placed in a pan with water and boiled. For example, two cups of *dush'-cut-duc-ka'* would be added to six cups of water and boiled. This could be eaten plain or mixed with dried or fresh beef.

At harvest time, sliced kernels of corn were fried or boiled as a dish for everyone participating in the harvesting and preservation of the corn. When the work of preservation was ended, the prepared corn was divided and shared by the several families that had participated.

An important consideration at this time was to keep back the best part of the yield for seed corn for the future. Each family held back two years' supply of seed corn every year, even in the twentieth century, against the possibility of drought. This was true of the "Indian" corn–red and blue–as well as the (yellow) sweet corn. The seed corn was placed carefully in the storage house. Corn for animals was shucked and stored in the barn. During this work period, the people enjoyed each other as well as the routine. It was a time of happy thoughts and excitement.

When the Hasinai came into this world, the women also carried the seed of the pumpkin, *coo-nooh-cah-ke-cus'-neh.* Like *kish-sih',* the Hasinai have retained it ever since, wherever they have traveled. When catkins appeared on the oak trees in the spring, it was time to plant pumpkins. They were planted in hills of earth, with four or five seeds placed in each hill. The ground was worked around each hill to keep the soil loose.

Pumpkins were gathered in the late summer or early fall. Many of them were stored whole. Others, which were to be dried, were left in the sun so that the walls would soften. The pumpkins were cut with a spiral stroke, slicing them from top to bottom. These strips were placed over a series of poles to dry in the sun. After they had reached the desired consistency, the strips were cut into shorter pieces. These were stored in sacks in the storage houses.

The word for pumpkin in Hasinai is *coo-nooh-cah-ke-cus'-neh,* which bears within it the verb form "to boil." In every case, the pumpkin was boiled with beef or pork as needed throughout the year. Sometimes pecans or hickory nuts were added to the mixture for variety in flavor and consistency. Nuts of whatever type were boiled for a long time prior to being added to the meat and pumpkin mixture. At other times, nuts were pounded in the *ki'-cooh* in the same manner as corn. Then the powder was added to the mix.

The best of the pumpkins were chosen for their seeds and saved for the future, just as with the corn. Even at the present time in the late twentieth century, Hasinai varieties of corn and pumpkin can be obtained in Oklahoma. Pumpkin seeds are stored in sacks and jars in the house or the barn.

Peas, *ca-key-dun-nay'-ah,* and beans, *dah-bus,* were also important to the diet. It was traditional to plant peas and corn in the same field. The peas were staked alongside the corn. Both peas and beans were planted and staked in the early spring after the last threat of a late frost. They were watched through the spring and early summer. As they ripened, they were picked and shelled. They were dried and stored in sacks as well. The *dah-bus* were similar to the black beans familiar throughout the American southwest. Together with peas, these were mainstays of the diet, adding valuable vegetable protein.

Three types of potatoes form part of the Hasinai vocabulary: *e'-ha-beh-tso,* sweet potato; *e'-ha-cah-yooh,* white potato; and *e'-ha-si-nai,* Indian (wild) potato, which is still found wild in northwestern Louisiana and eastern Texas. The last is a common starchy tuber, which produces a vine with white and purple flowers found in damp areas. Other vegetables were planted: beets, cabbage, and lettuce. These crops were rotated from field to field each year. Tradition indicated that everything grew better if moved from place to place. In the twentieth century most of these vegetables were planted from seeds purchased from feedstores. But corn and pumpkin were also produced from Hasinai varieties, as well as from commercial seed.

Domestic grapevines replaced the wild varieties that had supplied the Hasinai in earlier times. The grapes were eaten fresh and preserved. Melons and tomatoes supplemented the diet as well. Small orchards of peach and plum trees provided additional fruit.

These were dried or preserved as jelly. The fruit was cut into sections and dried on canvas in the same way as *dush'-cut-duc-ka'*. The pieces were turned twice a day. The process took from three to five days to complete. If the fruit or vegetables were not dried enough, they would mold and be ruined.

Agriculture was a principal way of life for the Hasinai well into the twentieth century, just as it had been throughout the history of the tribes. The technical aspects of farming changed little over the centuries. Comparison indicated that overall organization involving the village in clearing fields may have been somewhat more complex at an earlier period. Around each village, fields were made in the clearings. The soil was loosened with hand tools, very much like intensive forms of agriculture at the present time. Two crops of corn were sown in the earlier periods. The first was planted in April and the second in June. The first variety was a corn with a small stalk; it matured rapidly. The tall corn was planted later and was ready for harvesting by late July. So, in a period of four months, the Hasinai had two large crops of corn. Beans and peas were planted and staked in close proximity to corn, just as in twentieth-century practice. Preservation was essentially the same for corn, pumpkins, peas, and beans.[2]

In agriculture, overall Hasinai tradition taught that there was never a way to be false with the earth *and* survive. How one managed to do this always allowed for individual differences and new ways. Each individual was taught the responsibilities necessary for existence. In this way, children knew from an early age the difference between gain and loss in matters pertaining to the earth.

Emphasis was always put on careful observation, but not without intuitive judgment. Even where the economy of the twentieth-century southwest has changed drastically, principles taught by a close relationship with the earth hold value beyond common estimation. The ways of the Hasinai provided a sense of community, yet with knowledge that this in itself could not provide many alternative paths into the future.

FOUR

Duck Dance

ARCHITECTURE

The duck dance, *ka-kee-wee-dum'-mah,* translates as "dancing face to face." The singers with the drum are seated at the western edge of the dance ground. As the first song starts, pairs of men, side by side, come out toward the center. They dance facing forward with a double-step on each foot in a wide counterclockwise pattern. The women come in, each pair dancing backward, facing a pair of men. At the cue from the singers and a momentary change in tune and drum-beat about every minute, the leading pair of men steps around and in back of women in line. This procedure continues until the whole circle consists of alternating pairs, if there is an equal number of men and women. At each change, there are mirthful "quack-quacks" from the men. During one of these songs, usually the fourth, the men "let 'em through," by moving away laterally enough to let the women all continue dancing along between the two lines of men. At a cue from the singers near the end of this song, each pair of men moves back together in front of the pair of women close to them. The dance continues in this recurrent fashion.

In the twentieth century, vernacular forms of architecture, of white weatherboard construction, have replaced the traditional Hasinai housing styles that were once so familiar in the southwest. The only vestiges of the earlier style of living are the dance ground and the *cah-cah-say'-day-ah,* or arbor. Arbors are found near modern farm homes in some instances. Few Hasinai live in the traditional village community that prevailed through much of their history. Most Hasinai live in large urban communities or on their original allotment.[1]

Dance grounds are the central focus of Hasinai culture and learning, as they have been for centuries. The Whitebead Dance Ground is a level plaza in northern Caddo county. Around the central plaza are the wooded camp sites used by the Hasinai throughout the period of the dance cycle. The most frequently used dance ground is on tribal land immediately east of the Caddo Tribal Offices near Binger. It is a plaza surrounded by arbors, public buildings, and small family cabins. Both dance grounds are level areas that have been constructed along hill sides. An unusual dance space has been enclosed as a part of the Caddo office building. It has an earthen floor, but is roofed over and has masonry walls surrounding it.

The arbor is a popular structure still constructed near homes. It has a square or rectangular roof pattern. Peeled oak poles provide the support for the *coo'-ne-sah'-ne-coo-ah* (roof). This is built with a slight pitch extending away from a central ridge. The framework is lightweight but sturdy, usually made of willow. The sides are open to the air. These structures often last about two years. The ground around the arbor and the house is cleared. The ground was usually made into a hard pan to protect against fire and snakes.

A surprising amount of knowledge has been retained about traditional Hasinai architecture. Reproductions of traditional houses have been built on three sites in Texas and Oklahoma: at the Davis Site Park near Alto, Texas; at the Spiro Mound Site Park near Spiro, Oklahoma; and in Indian City in Anadarko, Oklahoma. Two basic methods of *cah-ha-ne-say'-ah* (house) construction are known, although rarely practiced. One is the log construction concept; the other is the domed grass house method. Important rediscoveries of classical and historical Hasinai centers in the 1920s and 1930s have provided additional information. Archeological investigations have also provided information about the classical dance grounds and ceremonial centers. Comparison of oral tradition and material cultural remains indicates continuity and balance even after the disruptions in the lives of the Hasinai in the modern period.

The log houses were constructed of large stakes placed in an upright position in a rectangular or square plan. The roof was thatched with long grass, tied in place on a wooden framework.

The only access was through a main doorway. There were no windows. A fireplace was placed normally at the center of the structure; in a traditional home, it was never extinguished, night or day.

The framework of the house consisted of two pairs of forked poles places upright in the ground at the four corners of the structure. Horizontal beams were tied in place to define the upper reaches of the walls of the house. Rising above these beams were the support rafters, which supported the peak. This formed a hip roof, with four slopes angling away from the peak pole. Additional rafters were tied into place along the longest slopes and from one side to the other across the structure to give the framework rigidity. The walls were made of heavy posts that were driven into the ground, very close together; no space was allowed between them. The pitch of the roof was very steep to insure rapid runoff of rain water.

The domed style of construction called for a completely thatched structure, from the ground to the highest point over the center of the living space. Construction began with the placement of a central timber. This was often notched to serve as a ladder. Then long poles were placed in the ground in a circle around the center pole. Using the center timber, the poles were tied together at the top, forming a dome. Willow rods were then interlaced across the poles, creating lathing for the thatch. In this method of building, as with the other, there was one door. It normally faced the east. After the exterior was finished, the central timber was removed.

Archeological evidence indicates that an earlier style of construction followed the lines of the log house style. It consisted of four plastered walls with a pyramidal roof. This had a square base with four slopes rising to a peak. The roof was supported by a complex system based on four central support beams and crossovers. The support walls were reinforced with vertical timbers. These were plastered over a wooden lath substructure with a kind of clay cement, which was fired when in place. Usually there was one entrance into the house from the east. A clay-shell hearth was placed in the center of the floor of the structure.[2]

In the later years of the classic period, rectangular began to predominate over square constructions. These apparently had gabled roofs with two slopes, usually of the same pitch. The support walls were of the same type of construction as in the earlier period. Interior support for the roof came from two large vertical beams that held a single roof timber in place. Interior walls were constructed of vertically placed timbers in both styles of housing. Construction provided for a prepared clay *cha-yun'-nah-hum* (floor), with a raised clay threshold at the entrance.

The classic villages and ceremonial centers were situated in close proximity to fresh running water. The *coo-num-me'-tah* (town) was surrounded by the fields that provided the agricultural abundance of the Hasinai. At a central plaza, the public meeting buildings, monuments, and community storage houses were constructed. Industry and planning became increasingly important as the complexities of life bound the villagers together in cooperative efforts. Balance and continuity were the foundational elements of community planning.

Architectural and artistic evidence of the classical culture has been collected from centers throughout the extended region of the Hasinai influence in the southwest. In the eastern and southern portions of the region, styles closely associated with the Mississippi River valley predominated in the ceramic pieces found in major population centers. But the area most closely associated with the Hasinai styles of engraving and design show a genius of their own. Elements of design unlike those of the cultures to the east appeared at the ceremonial center, commonly known as the Davis site, near Alto, Texas. This major mound complex and village site will be referred to as *Kee-wut'*, a contemporary term of reference. Its remains are in the *Cah-ye-tsi* or Neches River valley in what is now eastern Texas.

Kee-wut' is on a high alluvial terrace above an old stream bed about one mile north-northeast of the present course of the Neches in the heart of the Hasinai country. The remains of the urban complex extend over approximately sixty acres. The most prominent architechtural features are three large mounds constructed of earth, clay, and ash. Two of the mound structures are considered to be temple platforms. The third is defined as a burial mound. The archeological discoveries of this complex were made in the late 1930s and early 1940s under the supervision of Alex D. Krieger of the University of Texas at Austin. More recent work has been completed under the supervision of Dee Ann Story, also associated with the University of Texas at Austin.[3]

The largest of the temple mounds is L-shaped, with a flat-topped structure measuring about eighty-five meters in length and forty-five meters in maximum width. The second mound platform is approximately two hundred sixty meters to the northwest of the largest mound. It is rectangular and presently stands about two meters high, forty-five meters long, and twenty-eight meters wide. Approximately one hundred sixty meters north of the second temple mound is the burial mound. It is a conical structure about thirty meters long and twenty-three meters wide, and stands about five-and-one-half meters high. The south slope of the structure has an incline much less steep than that of the other sides.

The remains of houses and other material remains are concentrated around and between the mound structures. This includes the remains of pottery and stone implements. There are also objects of materials foreign to the area in and around *Kee-wut'*. These include objects of marine shell, copper, high quality flint, novaculite, and galena. They indicate far-flung trading relationships.

Numbers of Caddoan sites were worked and recorded in the 1930s in a systematic way. Included are the Gahagen and Sanders sites in the valley of the Red River, as well as the Roden site further upriver in the same valley. The most sensational discovery was that of the site near Spiro, Oklahoma, in the Arkansas River valley, which will be referred to as *Dit-teh,* also a contemporary reference. All of these sites were apparently nuclei for districts of comparatively large areas.[4]

Dit-teh was the largest of the sites of the *Kee-oh-na-wah'-wah* or the "Old People" (ancestors). Despite all the years of archeological work there, it has never been mapped completely. Only in the late 1970s were previously unrecognized structures identified on the extreme west of the site. Architecturally, the *Dit-teh* complex is dominated by two large monumental structures and a series of seven smaller mounds. The burial mound at the extreme eastern edge of the site is the largest in the urban complex. It measures approximately ninety-one meters in length, thirty-seven meters in width, and ten meters tall at its highest point.

Architectural features found within the mound structures include the primary mound, a clay basin area, a central chamber, and an earthen ramp extending northeast from the main structure. The platform mound in the western cluster around the plaza is about sixty meters long, fifty-three meters wide, and four-and-one-half meters high. The western group of mounds stands on a higher terrace than the burial complex, which is one level above the flood plain. In the period just prior to growing contact with European colonists and explorers, the large burial mound was capped with a conical shape. No more burials or mortuary building took place. There seemed to have been a concerted decision to stop using the structure. The mound cap was neatly finished. There were no signs of war or violence. In fact, there are no fortifications in evidence at either *Dit-teh* or *Kee-wut'*.

The architectural heritage of the Hasinai provides one of the most important bridges through which the generations from the ancestors to the present offer a sketch of a people in balance and peace. Estimation by material remains, however, is secondary to the importance of the Hasinai dance grounds at the Caddo Tribal Complex north of Anadarko, Oklahoma. In terms of cultural expression, living tradition provides a truer measure.

FIVE

Alligator Dance

CLOTHING

In the alligator dance, *kuh'-ho ka-oh'-shun,* the drum is taken slowly to the northwest edge of the dance arena while the two songs usually used in this dance are sung. The lead dancer appears with a growing line behind him of men alternating with women, holding hands, one behind the other. The dance movement is a quick trot with the leader shouting a loud "Yo-we-ho," with an answering chorus of "Ee-ho" from the line behind him, as he leads a serpentine course ending in a coiling counterclockwise turn around the drum. As the windup starts, the drummers begin singing the alligator dance songs; the line of dancers stops chorusing. Before the coil of dancers is wound too tightly around the drum, the leader starts unwinding the group and leads a meandering line around the dance ground with the chorus again taking over the singing as the drums fall silent. The dancers slowly walk to the northeast edge, where they stop. Then they approach the drum and wind around it, ending the chorus as the drummers again take up the song. This procedure is followed at the southeast and finally the southwest corner of the dance ground.

The introduction of trade cloth among the Hasinai by the French in the seventeenth century drastically changed the tradition in clothing and personal adornment. Thus, in the twentieth century, buckskin moccasins are the only material vestige of the ancient past. Other buckskin clothing, common in previous centuries, is rarely seen. The moccasins and the women's cloth dresses and ribboned headdress are the most distinctive traditional clothes.

Two particular styles for women's dresses are used for ceremonial occasions. The two-piece *nah-kee-cah'-sun* (dress) is distinctive because of the one-piece upper portion of the dress, which covers the shoulders and upper arms. The skirt is attached to a band the size of the waist. Traditionally this is full and is gathered at the waist band. The one-piece *nah-kee-cah'-sun* is gathered just above the bust line and again at the waist. Two or three ribbons are stitched at the yoke and around the cuffs of the long sleeves. The ribbons are the same color in both places. Married women button their dresses down the front; unmarried women button theirs down the back. Women normally wear an apron, which is tied in the back, over the skirt of the dress. The upper portion of the apron is gathered at the waist, as well. A small patch pocket is placed over the right hip area. Ribbons accent the bottom of the apron, as they do the yoke and the sleeves of the dress.

The most distinctive feature of the women's traditional clothing is the *dush'-tuh*, headdress. The hard top portion of the *dush'-tuh* always has a butterfly shape. The top of the *dush'-tuh* measures four-and-one-quarter inches across, and the bottom measures four-and-five-eighths inches in width. From the top to the bottom, it is seven-and-one-half inches. The headdress is shaped so that it narrows to just one-and-one-half inches across at a section that is three-and-one-half inches from the top. The headdress is covered with a single piece of black felt, edged with colored ribbon on both sides. Then it is beaded with white seed beads along the edges and decorated with silver studs in various patterns according to individual preference. Ribbons are connected at the bottom of the headpiece and flow down the woman's back. Usually, four layers of ribbons are stitched to a separate ribbon band across the top, which is in turn stitched to the board material. These ribbons, most often, are "water silk," sometimes solid colors and sometimes plaid. The ribbons run the distance from the back of the head to the hemline of the dress. *Cai'-coo-tze*, bells, are placed at the bottom for their pleasant sound and weight. A silver band is placed at the middle of the *dush'-tuh*, where it is tied to the hair. Worked shell, silver pieces, or mirrors are attached to the outside ribbon for added decoration, running down the back. The *dush'-tuh* is worn by women and girls most often for the turkey dance in the afternoon before the night's dancing. The graceful movements of the dance and the flowing ribbons are a beautiful sight.

The most distinctive part of the men's dress is the *nah-kee'-cah-son-shoo-we,* shirt. It is simple in design and execution. The basic measurement is the one from the shoulder to the waist. Twenty-two inches and above would make a large shirt; approximately eighteen inches would make for a medium shirt. Originally, Hasinai shirts were long, going down to the knees, but currently they usually end at the upper thigh. The basic measurement is multiplied by four for the body of the shirt. The sleeves are made from another piece, which is double the measurement. A hole is cut for the neck and a small round collar is fitted to the inner round edge. The material for the front of the shirt is pleated to about the waist and fitted with two ribbons at that point. Small pieces are cut from the waste for the cuff; they are two-and-one-half inches wide and then another inch is added for the ruffles. A ten by ten inch square of cloth is sewn under each sleeve where it is attached to the body of the shirt. A *hey'-nee-one'-tse* or neckerchief is usually worn over the small round collar.

The *wah-hee (koo'-toe-cah-ee-nun'-na)* or moccasins of the Hasinai are made entirely of soft leather, usually deerskin. They are made to fit the foot from one piece of worked leather, sewn over the toe and at the end of the heel. Once they are completed, they are rolled and stored without any decoration. When new moccasins are needed, they are beaded on the toe and edged with cloth on the flaps. Men's moccasins are beaded with a diamond shape. A flower shape is used on the toe of women's moccasins.

The Hasinai use several stitches for beading at the present time. The looped stitch is normally the type sewn on moccasins. It is one with the thread strung through four *nah-kim-be* or beads, then taken through the leather. Another stitch is the gourd stitch, which must use an even number of beads. Each bead is sewn separately to the previous ones. This stitching is used to enclose some object, such as a drum stick, a wand, or a round cigarette lighter. The loom stitch uses an uneven number of beads in a specified length. Most often, the loom stitch beads are then sewn to an object—a belt or blanket. Other exotic stitches are used in decorative objects such as necklaces.

There are historical records by European colonists that describe the earlier clothing of the Hasinai. These were left by numbers of Spanish and French in the seventeenth and eighteenth centuries. Among the most detailed are those by Friar Isidro Felix de Espinosa, Friar Juan Augustín de Morfí, and Pierre Margry.[1]

Most garments were made from tanned deerskin. Buffalo hide was used for colder weather. Women's dresses were made of soft deerskin, which were very dark as a result of the tanning process. These were made in two pieces, one garment over the shoulders and the second tied at the waist, hanging to the ankles. The borders were lined with small white beads. Women's hair was described as combed and braided. Usually the hair was tied with a small cord of rabbit skin. Today the most prominent ornaments worn in the hair are *sue'-nah,* silver combs. Other personal items include *nah-kee'-nah-sin-cha* (bracelets of German silver), *nah-kee-tsu'-wit* (earrings), *cus-see-nah-kim'-be* (a beaded necklace). During the dances, the women also carry *cah-wah-sin'-neeh,* shawls, which are of light wool with long fringe, and *nah-kin-oon'-uh-nah,* fans, made from the feathers of hawks or sometimes waterfowl such as swans.

Glass has completely replaced all other substances for beads used in previous centuries. Necklaces of numerous strands of beads of the same color are used by the women in ceremonial dress to complement the colors of the dress, apron, and shawl. Earlier types of beads were made from mussel or conch shells. They were made in different shapes and sizes. The smaller ones were round and white. They were valued more than the larger sizes. Just as is presently true, the women wore numbers of strands at a time. Where presently women wear silver earrings, earlier it is reported that women wore ones made of the core of a great spiral-shaped sea shell.

Everyday dress varied with the season. Little clothing for the children and the men was the normal manner of dress in the summer. Shirts, leggings, and moccasins were worn in the cooler seasons. Additional outer clothing was worn in the winter. Just as today, everyday clothing was used for its durability, whereas ceremonial occasions called for the finest garments that a person possessed. The posture of the individual was important despite the occasion. Both men and women dressed and continue to dress with decorum. Today, however, only the ceremonial clothing distinguishes the Hasinai from anyone else.

Traditional clothing remains the outward sign of the Hasinai culture. These personal items are often made by relatives. They are handed on from generation to generation with the ways of thinking that provide the alternatives necessary for the preservation of Hasinai civilization in the American southwest. Clothing and other items are cared for with pride in one's heritage. They are not barriers to ways of thinking and action, but the representation of time-honored forms of behavior.

SIX

Women's Dance

FAMILY RELATIONSHIPS

Singers with the drum begin on the western edge of the dance ground. They start the first of many fine songs, as women begin lining up facing the drum. They stand and sing along with the drummers through about a dozen songs. During the last two of these songs, there are parts when the drummers fall silent and the women sing alone. With the next four or five songs, the women dance a few steps backward and then forward, moving away from and back to the drum.

Then the dancers start in a line, moving in a counterclockwise direction. They circle the center of the arena with a two-step with each foot. Many songs later, in the last phase of the dance, the men join in, each facing his chosen partner, dancing backward, until the cue from the drum signals a 180-degree turn of each pair. Then the woman is dancing backward, reversing again at the next change, and so on to the final, very fast, song.

This dance, late at night, often seems long and boring to young children. Many Hasinai remember going to sleep with these songs lulling them after a long night of play with their friends around the dance ground.

Among the Hasinai, the basis of all social organization rests clearly in the family. Relationships are bound up in the names of individuals and the vocabulary for relatives, who are known to each person born into the body of the people. These words of relationship have power in themselves. The name of a person is never told outside the family. A personal name holds the most power of all. It should not be used.

Of these relationships, the most important are those of the *ah-ah* or father and the *e'-nah* or mother. From these two parents grows a fabric of well-being that provides security in the world. Immediately, the *cah-yo'-tsi* or baby finds basic links with the generation that preceded that of the parents. These include the *e'-but* or grandfather on the male side and *e'-kah* or grandmother on the male side of the family. On the female side, the grandfather is *ah-ah-e-nah,* and the grandmother is the *e-nah-ha-ee-may.* The child if a boy is *ah'-kin* (son); a girl is *hay-in* or daughter. In the same generation, a younger brother is known as *tu'-we-ti-ti,* and the older brother is *kee-nee-ti-ti.* A younger sister is *tay-ti-ti,* and an older sister is referred to as *e-a'-ti-ti.* These relationships are the most critical of all that a person has. Of the two sides of the family, the maternal is the more critical in establishing all other relationships.

Among the more important relatives for a child are the aunts and uncles. The *ah-ah e'-may* is an older uncle on the male side of the family; an *ah-ah ti-ti* is a younger uncle on the male side. An older uncle on the female side is referred to as *e-nay e'-may* and a younger uncle on the same side of the family as the *e-nay-ti-ti.* An older aunt on the male side is an *ah-hey;* a younger aunt is *ah-hey'-ti-ti.* On the female side, an older aunt is *e-nah-e'-may* and the young one an *e'-nah-ti-ti.* Even more distantly, ancestors were *key-un-nooh wah'-wah ha-e-may'-che*—literally, "a lot of persons way back there."

Traditional understanding of marriage and the basis of family life lie within these close ties. The persons most closely associated with an individual through these relationships would normally help to decide the marriage relationship. On occasion an arranged marriage was made for a man and a woman. But most often, when a couple was formally united for the purpose of living together with continuing responsibilities, it was their unique choice. The most important concern by all connected with the marriage was not to marry within the extended family. So even though there was always this tight network of family surrounding the individual, there was always also the pressure to seek relationships outside close blood ties. As a person grew to maturity within the family, there was little or no sense of rebellion against the directions of the family. There was usually no thought of questioning this authority.

If for some reason disruption of the immediate family occurred, through either death or separation, custom helped to bridge this temporary lack of order. For example, if the wife died, the sister of the dead woman came and took over the home and the children. If there was a divorce, the children went with the mother. She was always the primary arbitrator of discipline for the children in daily living and tribal relationships. For example, the *e-nah* saw that the children did not beat on the drum, or ask a lot of questions, or play in the dance area during tribal gatherings. It was considered important to teach the young, but within the family sphere. For instance, while gathering herbal medicine, a child would want to know about the plants and the reason why the herbs were replaced by tobacco. An explanation would be given by the *e'-nah* or *e'-nah-ha-ee-may* that the tobacco was returning a gift to *Ah-ah-ha'-yo* for the gift of healing.

Often the young were expected to know the answer to questions before they had been told anything. Intuition played an important role in everyone's education.

One of the most interesting roles among the Hasinai is that of the teaser. Jesting is a way of helping individuals to keep their perspective and not to take everything too seriously. In this manner, a young person or an adult of many years is buffeted by good humor. It is a matter of providing a sense of balance within the close relationships of the family. Sarcasm is an extreme form of this type of humorous play. Other forms may be sexual or satirical in nature. Teasing sharpened the wit and provided many instances of good-natured fun.

While growing to maturity, the child was taught that he or she did not simply take up space on earth, but filled it to the benefit of all the people. In life, happiness was to be found within one's self, coming through relationships throughout a lifetime. It was also taught that the trouble that anyone had to face could allow that person to grow emotionally. Otherwise, problems would destroy the individual. Individuals could use worry to destroy themselves if they chose. It was always emphasized that nothing confronting a person was so powerful that he or she could not handle the difficulty. The key was to accept the discipline of moderation and balance in all things.

Even the boarding school regimentation enforced by the United States government was acceptable to Hasinai children in the twentieth century according to this line of reason. The greatest difficulty was that the loving element was missing from those responsible for operating the schools for the federal government. It was learned that even this could be overcome to some extent by the sense of community among the students. In Oklahoma many tribes were represented in the boarding schools. Tribal differences were important, but were not barriers. For instance, most tribes instilled a strong sense of personal property in the young. No one used things that belonged to others. This feeling was so strong that individuals did not have to keep their things under lock and key. Also, as at home, if an older child asked someone younger to do something, it was never questioned by the younger child.

In the vast majority of cases, the young among the Hasinai would leave home reluctantly and would return to a loving welcome. They all knew their relatives. But in the twentieth century, the changing economic situation and technological innovations in transportation have separated the people, diminishing the closeness of family contact and the fabric of traditional Hasinai culture. There are no rites of passage from one stage of life to another. It is increasingly difficult to hold onto what is Hasinai—what is Caddo. There is greater and greater loss of song and dance. Spiritual emphases cannot be passed on to the young in the day-to-day traditional ways as in even the recent past. It is said that all too often the Hasinai throw away the good to accept the new, no matter what it may do to them.

Hasinai sense of spirituality is like corn and pumpkin: it must be nurtured. The spiritual core can exist only with great difficulty in the chaos that surrounds it. Yet many Hasinai still say, "Don't worry; our time will come." Many travel regularly from Kansas, Texas, Mexico, and from places throughout Oklahoma to the tribal dance grounds at the Caddo Tribal Complex near Binger to renew themselves. Among the older Hasinai there remains a strong sense of peace. The flow of existence is comforting and good. Change is not especially noticeable.

Comparison with published materials on the Hasinai indicates very little change in family relationships.[1] Legalistic concerns of state governments have affected marriage relationships. Separation and divorce are the areas where change is most evident. Marriage was more tenuous among the Hasinai in the eighteenth and nineteenth centuries. Separation did not carry the stigma and emotional impact that has been imposed in contemporary America. It was simply a matter of husband and wife collecting their personal possessions and leaving. Custom dictated which material objects and possessions belonged to either of the two individuals. There was no public display of bitterness or jealousy; that was beneath the standards of appropriate behavior. Separation and divorce were managed with the least possible disruption of the community.

In all matters, the family was the carrier of Hasinai tradition. The families were the inner core of the blood ties that made for the strength of the Hasinai. This support was critical to the individual's ability to deal with the natural flow of existence. Loyalties extended through the family were recognized by all. The claims of morality upon the people were to support the best within the individual. True relationships are of the *ha-no-coo'-ah-yah* or soul. In Hasinai, the term for body is *coo-ah-nee'-yah*–literally, "carrier of the soul." Spiritual ties reach across space and time to strengthen the individual. At the present time, prophetic understanding is all but drowned out by material changes. The balance between the spiritual and the material must be regained. Too much emphasis on one or the other within the family sphere would portend an even worse age to come.

SEVEN

Stirrup Dance

TRIBAL RELATIONSHIPS

The drum and singers are placed on the west side of the dance ground. Pairs of men and women face each other, with the males on the right and the females opposite the males. The dancers start in a quick trot, circling counterclockwise around the arena. Each pair holds hands throughout the dance. They all hold the right hand of the partner with their right hand and the left with their left. Upon a cue from the singers, when changing songs, the woman places her right foot lightly over the man's raised left foot and they hop along on one foot each. At the cue, changing from the *Ya nay hay' ka way ah* song to the *No ha way* song, they change places and start the quick trot again, until the change, again assuming the stirruplike hop on one foot. In the past, a cue was given during the hopping phase to twirl around in a 360-degree turn. Just a moment or two is given to each phase, with much fun and laughing as the dancers become exhausted and trip as the dance draws to an end.

In the twentieth century, the Indian Reorganization Act of 1934 and its application to the Oklahoma tribes in the Oklahoma Indian Welfare Act of 1936 were recognized as a watershed. Between 1937 and 1942, when the involvement in global conflict drew federal attention away from domestic affairs, eighteen units of Indian government organized under the law in Oklahoma. These ranged in size from Creek tribal towns to entire nations.

The law provided that any recognized tribe or band of Indians residing in Oklahoma had the right to adopt a constitution and bylaws in order to organize as a whole for the benefit of tribal members. A federal charter provided that the tribe could administer credit, operate production marketing efforts, and provide for consumer protection, as well as land management. On January 17, 1938, the Caddo people, including the Hasinai, the Kadohadacho, and the Natchitoche, organized under the law. Commissioner of Indian Affairs John Collier issued a charter that took effect with the consent of a majority vote of the people enrolled or recognized as Caddo in November of 1938.

The Caddo Constitution provided for a governing body for the Caddo tribe in Oklahoma, which was named the Caddo Council, consisting of a chairman, vice-chairman, secretary-treasurer, and two councilmen. It was to meet the first Tuesday of each month, with annual meetings of the tribe in June of each year. The chairman would be the chief parliamentary leader in a system closely resembling that of the British government. In addition to establishing this form of governance to deal more effectively with that of the United States, Section 1 of Article X, stated: "All members of the Caddo Indian Tribe shall enjoy without hinderance [*sic*], freedom of worship, conscience, speech, press, assembly, and association." Although these rights had been extended to all American Indians in 1924, this was the first time they had been given to the Hasinai by name.

The charter clearly demarcated the limits of tribal action within the federal system. It defended and safeguarded the rights and powers of the Caddo within clearly defined limits, empowering the chairman and the council:

> To promote in any way the general welfare. To advance the standard of living of the Tribe through development of tribal resources, the acquisition of new tribal land, the preservation of existing land holdings, the better utilization of land and the development of a credit program for the Tribe.

As defined in the Cherokee cases of 1831 and 1832 American Indian tribes functioned as "domestic dependent nations" within the influence of federal jurisdictional limits. This reform legislation recognized the sovereign status of the tribal entities. The Caddo Council established a means through which the Caddo tribe could work for the betterment of its tribal members in concert with the government of the United States.

Hasinai traditional government had worked for its people in tribal and international affairs for centuries in the southwest. The new Caddo Council was an acceptable reform recognized by both the United States and the Hasinai. The traditional government was altered at various times through the years to meet new circumstances. Yet the basic framework remained much the same well into the twentieth century. The upheavals of the series of forced removals in the nineteenth century had taken its toll on the government. The Hasinai had settled finally in Indian Territory. There the major subdivisions were communities in the areas of Anadarko, Binger, Fort Cobb, and Gracemont (all in Oklahoma).

In the period of the creation of the territory and state of Oklahoma, these four communities had recognized headmen and elders, who represented their respective peoples in the unified Hasinai tribal system. The Hasinai were headed by a principal leader or *cah-de*. The men who held this position included: Caddo Jake (1890–1902), Whitebread (1902–1913), Enoch Hoag (1913–1920), Harry Edge (1920–1922), Amos Longhat (1922–1923), and Charles Adams (1923–1937). These men were qualified for the role of *cah-de* by their hereditary position among the Hasinai and the general acceptance of their leadership by the people. The *cah-de* presided over the general meetings of the Hasinai *cah-nah-ha* or headmen and other elders from the communities in Oklahoma. The principal role of the *cah-de* was to insure that each of the *cah-nah-ha* and elders had an opportunity to be heard. In this manner, all points of view could be expressed before any decision was made. The welfare of the tribe remained uppermost in the minds of all present.

The meetings of the Hasinai leaders were long, with anyone among the Hasinai people free to come and be in attendance. At all times, the spiritual nature of the work of the tribe was at the center of deliberations. Often ceremonial considerations were of prime concern. At other times, civil matters were uppermost in the work of the *cah-de* and elders. At no time, however, did the United States government recognize this legitimate government of the Hasinai people.

The acceptance of the federally chartered form of governance in 1938 was a major watershed. The people looked to the Caddo tribal council, led by the elected chairman or *nit-tso-sah-dos-cha-ah*, which literally means "one who takes the chair," for leadership in a new sense henceforth. From this point on, there was confusion among the people as to the roles of the *nit-tso-sah-dos-cha-ah* and the *cah-de*. This complex knot of traditional and imposed forms of government and leadership finally came under great tension with the relatively large infusion of money and programs in the 1970s.

Melford Williams, who had the family ties and the traditional training of the Hasinai *cah-de*, was elected to the position of *nit-tso-sah-dos-cha-ah* in 1968. Taking advantage of the challenge of "self-determination" by the federal government, Williams and the council instituted a period of reform of the chartered government. In the late 1960s, the Caddo Tribe of Oklahoma instituted one of the first Indian housing programs in the nation. In 1969 Williams became the first chairman of the Oklahoma Indian Housing Committee Association, which was established by representatives of the federally recognized Indian tribes in Oklahoma.

In other areas of concern, the Caddo Council moved decisively. An important effort toward reform touched on the possibility of amending the tribal charter of 1938. Because the Caddo Council had to operate in many new and more sophisticated directions in relation to an expanding number of U.S. government agencies, more flexibility and relative power were needed. The reform change provided that the Caddo executive committee or council could propose amendments to the Constitution under the charter by a simple majority vote. It also allowed for initiative proposals supported by at least fifty members of the Caddo tribe of Oklahoma. After either of these first steps, the proposed amendment would be taken to the Secretary of the Interior for approval. Then a vote was taken on the proposed amendment by the enrolled members of the tribe. This reform amendment was agreed to and in place in 1970.

A second reform measure was the effort to tighten control of the tribal council over the Bureau of Indian Affairs (BIA) authority to lease trust lands. Not only were Caddo lands being leased to non-Indians at low rental rates, but trust lands were being lost to tribal members at a consistent rate. The federal government had assumed the trust relationship for the benefit of tribal members. But all too often leases enforced by the BIA read as if they were written for the benefit of the parties who were leasing the land and to the detriment of the Caddo people. A measure correcting the leasing agreements was passed, but it failed to curtail the loss of trust lands to the degree that was hoped.

In the council report of 1970, the executive committee favored "direct education in both areas [academic and vocational] with parallel emphasis at the equal pace into both cultures [Hasinai and Anglo-American] so that students are provided a choice in academic or vocational, as well as both cultures." To Williams and the council, cultural concerns were central to a realistic education for Caddo youth. The health of the people depended upon those ways of thinking that were native Hasinai as much or more than upon West European colonial concepts and technical thought. In an effort to approach these cultural matters systematically, material culture was taught in training projects. Caddo language classes were supported by the tribe in recognition that the heart of the culture was reflected in its language.

In the early 1970s, Williams was defeated in a reelection attempt. At this point, the roles of *nit-tso-sah-dos-cha-ah* and *cah-de* again became distinct. The people still came to Williams for traditional concerns. In 1975 the Hasinai Cultural Center was organized by representatives in Oklahoma, Texas, and Kansas to provide a modern corporate form for tribal activities. Its stated objectives were to "develop and save Caddo lands, customs, music, crafts, and traditions. . . . To encourage our youth to maintain a strong interest in their tribal values and . . . to study and preserve the Caddo language, dances, and history." Williams served as the head of these Hasinai efforts until his death in 1978.

The disruptive conditions brought on by hegemony of the United States in Hasinai affairs has distorted the traditional form of government. The role of the *nit-tso-sah-dos-cha-ah* has been reduced, at times, to simply carrying program agreements back from Washington, D.C., rather than championing the position of the tribe. Over the centuries the Hasinai had developed a stable system of governance. W. W. Newcomb, Jr., wrote:

> What we know of the Caddoes' political organization is much more intelligible to people of Western civilization than that of many other Texas Indians. This is not because it closely resembles modern democracies or other political systems, but because it was a bureaucracy, containing a series of graded offices—and officers, each with specific duties to perform.[1]

All colonial accounts of the Hasinai indicate the importance of a spiritual ruler, who was referred to as the *see'-neeh-tsi.* This was a hereditary position that bound the people to the Hasinai destiny. The male heir symbolized, in his person, the community of the Hasinai people. The heads of the tribes were *cah-de*s. They, too, inherited their role. However, acceptance by the people was necessary for them to function in the position. For example, in the twentieth century, Enoch Hoag instructed his children in the history and ethics of the Caddo people to train them for leadership. He wanted his son Clarence to follow him as *cah-de,* but the people did not accept him in that role. A second son, Robert Hoag, acted the part of the *cah-de,* but was ignored by the people. Instead the people looked to a new line. In time Harry Edge assumed the role.

In the preremoval period, the tribes were often large enough that there were a number of subordinate headmen or *cah-na-ha*s. Each community had a *cah-na-ha* in the leadership role to provide for local leadership and to insure that the village had a representative in reaching tribal decisions. Each village also had a "town cryer" or *tum'-mah* to insure that everyone had full knowledge of the direction of tribal decisions and participated in the actions of the people. Currently, the *tum'-mah* is most prominent at the Caddo dances, where he insures the active participation of everyone present.[2]

In addition to the family ties and the unity of the tribe through accepted forms of leadership, the binding force in terms of community and spirituality is found in song and dance. One of the most important songs that bind the people together is the flag song. It shows honor and respect for the veterans of all the wars. The Caddo flag song ceremony is usually performed after the turkey dance in the late afternoon. The headman or a lead singer calls out the names of two veterans or warriors to come to the drum.

The two men walk in step from the drum to the flagpole. Everyone stands up to face the flag as the singers start the song. After lowering the flag, it is carefully folded, then returned to the drum. It is handed to the owner, usually a veteran's widow, who has received it after a military funeral service. The singers continue the song until the flag has been retrieved and folded.

Divisions among the Caddo have affected the civil life of the people. Some of these stresses have been introduced as religious reform. An important spiritually oriented dance that came to the Caddo from the Arapaho people in 1890 was the ghost dance. This dance is rarely done by the Hasinai in the post–World War II period. Usually the lead is taken by two or three singers who know some of the many songs from the past. The singers, facing east, start on the west side of the dance ground. The first singer carries a hand-held drum. As the first song is started, those who want to dance line up side by side to the right of the lead singer. Usually men and women alternate in the dance line. About a minute after the song starts, all hold hands and start sidestepping to the left, following a circular clockwise pattern. The steps are very short and usually rapid, done in time with the song and drum. The dancers move very slowly as a group. The leader correlates the number of dancers and the circle radius, so that the song ends just after he reaches the starting point. With many persons dancing, the song may end after the leader has traveled halfway around the circle. There is a significant stop between songs when the leader reaches the east side. The next song then takes him to the west side starting-point. Those older ones who still know and like the songs and the spiritual meaning of the dance are the first to join the dancers. They like to accompany the singing, even though it takes considerable physical effort.

Frank Whitebead, who passed away in 1978, traveled with Hadibuh, a headman in the Fort Cobb area, and other tribal members to learn about the ghost dance when it was introduced into Indian Territory in 1890. They crossed the South Canadian River at Caddo Jake's Crossing and traveled to Darlington. There they spent several days with the Cheyenne and some Arapaho ghost dance leaders. As it was taught at that time, the new religion demanded peaceful living as the only way to restore the benefits of life. The

Drummers at tribal dance. *Courtesy Phillips Collection, Western History Collections, University of Oklahoma Library*

Ralph Muro talking with the elders while women dance around them. *Courtesy Phillips Collection, Western History Collections, University of Oklahoma Library*

Ladies' choice dance. From left: Bedoka, Mellie Balkstar, unknown, and Willie Weller. *Courtesy Phillips Collection, Western History Collections, University of Oklahoma Library.* BELOW: Women cooking a meal at a tribal dance. *Courtesy Phillips Collection, Western History Collections, University of Oklahoma Library*

Stomp dance. *Courtesy Phillips Collection, Western History Collections, University of Oklahoma Library.* BELOW: Alice Cussen's dance costume. *Courtesy Phillips Collection, Western History Collections, University of Oklahoma Library*

Announcer at a tribal dance. *Courtesy Phillips Collection, Western History Collections, University of Oklahoma Library*

Alice Cussen at dance. *Courtesy Phillips Collection, Western History Collections, University of Oklahoma Library*

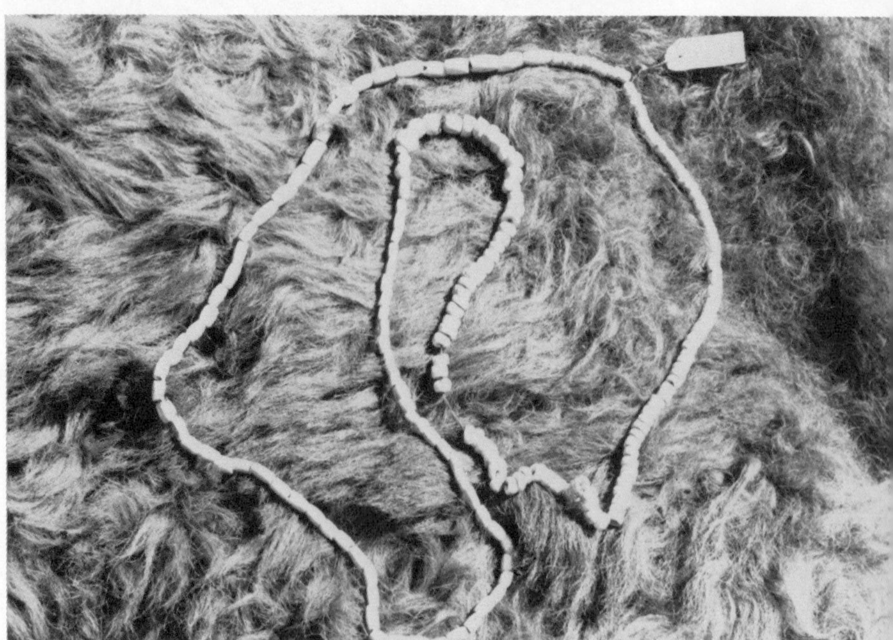

Traditional Caddo bell rattle for bell dance. BELOW: Beads from Spiro Mound Complex.

Traditional split cane stick dice. BELOW: Lead singer Wimpy Edwards and other singers at Caddo Dance Ground, 1987.

Washaniki phase of the turkey dance, Caddo Complex Dance Ground, 1987. The man at center is Donnie Frank, present Caddo tribal chairperson.

Turkey dancers at Whitebead Dance Ground. Vynola Newkumet is at far right, facing the camera.

From left: Lizzie Williams, Vynola Newkumet, Terry Newkumet, and Stella Beaver.

songs and the religious practice were introduced among the Caddo at Caddo Jake's place and then at Whitebead's place.

The ghost dance pole or *ee-cha'* was an important part of the dance. It was about twelve feet in length, always set up in the center of the dance ground, where it was circled by the dancers. In the beginning, no drum was used by the Caddo singers, but the small hand drum was soon introduced. The Hasinai began to compose and use their own songs. These were drawn from visions received in trances. John Wilson was one of the first among the Caddo to receive such a vision. A few old Cheyenne and Arapaho songs are still retained in the Hasinai song series. It remains a powerful means of expression among the Hasinai, but respected by only a few older persons.

The ghost dance theology brought about divisions within the tribe and among families among the Caddo people in Oklahoma. In this way it is like the Native American Church. This new theology has to do with peyote and indicates a new way for spiritual outlet for the Caddo. Peyote has been used by the Caddo for centuries, but the Native American Church has organized it in a new and forceful way. The ghost dance, the Native American Church, and the various Christian denominations have introduced new forms of division among the people.

Social dances without theological themes continue to strengthen the bonds of tribal life. One among these is the fish dance or *ka-key-wee'-ny be*—literally, "dancing sideways." In this dance, the singers with a drum are seated on the west side of the dance ground. When they start the first song, the women start off in single file. They dance in a circular counterclockwise pattern of overall movement, with a quick single step. At each cue from the singers the dancers change from facing half-right to half-left, and back to half-right, continuing in this fashion. In the last three songs, there are a few seconds of change in tempo of the song and the drum, when the women dance in place, with a slight backward and forward movement.

The stomp dance or *ha-ya-no-na-ee'-shish-na,* meaning "shake shells," is a popular social dance among the Hasinai. It is danced late in the night sequence. Some of the Hasinai women and girls are expert shell-shakers. A few Caddo men are good leaders, having learned short songs and answering choruses at the Muscogee-Creek or Yuchi dance grounds. Another dance introduced from outside the tribal framework but enjoyed in the modern period is the modern version of the war dance or fancy dance. The usual participants in the fast war dance are the young men and boys, as well as occasional girls, who are active in intertribal powwow activities. When the slow war dance is performed, many of those present join in the clockwise circle with the costumed war dancers leading. Another version is the straight dance, which is slower and more dignified. Even the older men join this. No feather bustles and other decorations of the fancy dance are used in the straight dance. Even young boys and toddlers are encouraged to join this dance, with special songs of praise. Though the Hasinai have adapted the present forms of war dance from the adjoining Plains tribes, they compose and use their own songs. These are danced shortly after the drum dance, which begins the night sequence of Caddo dances.

There are many Christian hymns or church songs that are important to the Hasinai. Many are Hasinai-language versions of well-known hymns. Others are original Caddo compositions. These were used in the area when English was an unfamiliar, secondary language. In translation, they may confound the Christian missionary. One contained the line, "Jesus threw a rock and away he ran." This was an interpretation of "Jesus is a Rock in a Holy Land." Some of the hymns are heard when friends praise the memory of a deceased friend or relative. The effort is always to try to find ties among all Hasinai, living and dead.

The Hasinai people had been settled for centuries in the region between the Red and Trinity Rivers. Their stable government involved all the people of the various allied tribes. The integrity of the Hasinai system was not seriously challenged until the beginning of the nineteenth century. Only when two European colonial systems began to infiltrate into the region did it begin to deteriorate. In the west, the Spanish established settlements in the Neches and Angelina river valleys near Nacogdoches as well as at Los Adaes on the Red River. To the east, the French established a trading post at Natchitoches on the Red River. These were tolerated by the Hasinai as active commercial centers for the exchange of goods.

The Hasinai preferred trading with the French throughout the eighteenth century.[3]

Political realism among the Hasinai is the very embodiment of faith in continuity and reason. This realism holds that through the calculations of tribal interests, leadership can maintain order against the anarchy created by the succession of moves by European colonial powers. Thereby, the Hasinai have moderated, where possible, the conflicting results brought on by the hegemony of the United States government in the nineteenth and twentieth centuries. It is with the hope that the United States can learn to be more enlightened in its understanding of its own interests that the Hasinai leadership continues to negotiate. In all eras there have been mature societies that have been moved by considerations of justice toward other societies. The Hasinai have sought this role as they have dealt with a succession of European colonial powers, including Spain, France, Mexico, Texas, and the United States. History has taught the risk of misplaced trust, as well as the benefits of cooperation.

EIGHT

Quapaw Dance

FOREIGN RELATIONSHIPS

The singers take the drum and start a slow walk counterclockwise around the arena. They are followed by pairs of men, side by side. Pairs of women precede the singers, dancing backward in front of the drum. At each cue from the singers during the song and at the end of each song, the leading pair of women separates to come around the drum and close in again before the leading pair of men. The next change brings the pair of women around the first pair of men to dance in front of the next pair of men. At the same time, the second pair of women comes around to dance with the first pair of men. This movement continues through all of the pairs. If there is a short line of men, the women dance past the first pair of men and around to join the women closer to the drum.

The foreign relationships of the Hasinai with other American peoples has always been dynamic. In Oklahoma, the relationships between the Hasinai and other tribes have been respectful and peaceful. Some associations have been influenced by geographic and administrative dictates. For example, the Wichita and the Delaware peoples live in close proximity to the Hasinai. In addition, the Bureau of Indian Affairs of the United States government has attempted to have the Caddo Tribe of Oklahoma work in concert with the two other tribes. Other close relationships have been affected by spiritual concerns. An example is the relationship with the Arapaho people through participation in the ghost dance ritual since 1890. Often the Hasinai invite the Shawnee and the Kickapoo to their dance ground. In turn, they dance at the other tribes' dance grounds on different occasions. Intermarriage by Hasinai and members of the Delaware tribe, and increasingly with members of the Kiowa tribe, has become more acceptable since World War II.

Relationships between the United States and the Caddo confederacy are dominated by the hegemony of the former over the latter. This is extremely important in political and economic matters of mutual concern. Formal ties with the United States are colored by a long history ranging back in time with the Republic of Texas, the Mexican Republic, France, and the Spanish empire in America. Even at the present time, relationships with the French are remembered as preferable to all the others. In the twentieth century, the intermarriage of Hasinai with Anglo-Americans is affecting ways of working together.

The closest relationships have always been within the Caddo confederacy including the Kadohadacho alliance and the Kiamichi to the north in the region of the Red River. These relationships have continued to remain strong, because of the blood ties and the incorporation of these peoples into the Caddo Tribe of Oklahoma. The same remains true of relationships with the Natchitoche alliance, farther down the Red River valley. There were strong relationships in earlier centuries with the Akokisa and Atakapa peoples who live along the Gulf Coast. Each year the Hasinai traditionally visited these peoples on the coast in the month of May, when the turtles laid their eggs. The Hasinai maintained an inviolable peace with these peoples, as did they with the confederacy.

Although the Hasinai traditionally sought peaceful solutions to problems, hostile relationships prevailed with certain tribes. In previous centuries the traditional enemies on the east were the Choctaw. This tribe with their allies, the Chickasaw raiders, harassed the eastern Caddo tribes. Osage raiders from the north disrupted civilized life on the Red River frontier. On the western plains, the historic enemies of the Hasinai were the Wichita and the Tonkawa. In the modern period, Apache raiders brought added danger to the western frontier.

At present, these historical relationships are recalled with good humor. Hasinai singers have removed from the turkey dance sequence some songs recalling military victories over the Choctaw and the Osage. This was done so that no one would be embarrassed when Choctaw and Osage members attended Caddo dances.

Hasinai relationships with European colonists have produced the greatest body of comparative literature. Most often, the written documentary evidence reflects the policy considerations of the colonial government, whether Spanish, French, or Anglo-American, in the cases of the Republic of Texas and the United States. Among the most informative are Herbert Eugene Bolton's *Texas in the Middle of the Eighteenth Century* (Berkeley: University of California Press, 1915); William Joyce Griffith's *The Hasinai Indians of East Texas as Seen by Europeans, 1687–1772* (New Orleans: Middle American Research Institute, Tulane University, 1954); and Elizabeth A. H. John's *Storms Brewed in Other Men's Worlds: The Confrontation of Indians, Spanish, and French in the Southwest, 1540–1795* (College Station: Texas A&M University Press, 1975). The movement to Indian Territory in 1859 is chronicled in Kenneth F. Neighbours' *Indian Exodus: Texas Indian Affairs, 1835–1859* (Quannah: Northtex Press, 1973). These volumes provide the history of the colonial patterns of expansion and retreat in the southwest in the modern period relying upon sources other than those of the Hasinai.[1]

In the late seventeenth century and throughout the eighteenth century, the Hasinai provinces were the focal point of colonial efforts by the Spanish and the French. These events began the process that profoundly changed Hasinai relationships to others and among themselves. At the beginning of this period, the principal tribes of the Hasinai confederation included Nabedache, Nabiti, Nacachua, Nacao, Nacogdoche, Nacono, Nadaco, Nasoni, Nechai, Neche, and Hainai. The province of Texas was named using the Hasinai word for "friends," *ta'-sha (tay-sha).* To both the Spanish and the French, the Hasinai were the preeminent nation in the region from the Mississippi River valley to the Rio Grande valley.

The Spanish way of attracting Indians to a Spanish lifestyle did not succeed among the Hasinai. In the Americas, the Spanish had successfully attracted many Indian peoples to mission stations through the introduction of stable agricultural production. But the Hasinai produced surpluses. In agricultural terms, their systems were superior to those of the Spanish. In addition, conversion to Christianity was directly tied to acceptance of Hispanic culture, which proved to be unacceptable as well. Most scholars, including the early Franciscans, blamed the failure of the missions on the strength of the Caddo traditional spirituality. Elsewhere in the Americas–Mexico, the Yucatan, the Andes–the Spanish had used military coercion for successful, permanent occupation. However, the Spanish military was ineffective in this region.

The French system, in contrast, was organized on a much more flexible basis. Trade goods, which became increasingly important to the Hasinai, were in more plentiful supply from the French. The Hasinai had acquired horses in sufficient numbers so that they were able to trade them, in addition to the furs and pelts that the French sought in the early eighteenth century. In return, the Hasinai obtained manufactured textiles, metal knives, hatchets, muskets, as well as ornamental objects. Iron tools, particularly knives and hoes, of French origin became increasingly important to trade relationships. In this way, the extension of European trade rivalries in the Hasinai territory was of profound significance in the lives of the people. Material innovations of European origin brought about a change in Hasinai life, which was then in economic decline.[2]

In addition to the changes brought by trade, European diseases took an increasing toll on the Hasinai people. Infectious diseases spread on an epidemic scale in 1691 and 1777, carrying off thousands of persons. There was a continual decline in population accompanied by a deterioration of order brought on by the chaos of revolution and war. It was truly a deplorable age.[3]

Changes in the hegemony of the southwest came repeatedly in the late eighteenth and early nineteenth century. Of the various colonial parties, the Spanish were the most hospitable of those who held sway in the region. In turn, the Mexican government offered all the Caddo refuge in the province of Texas.

As a result of the recurring pressures from the United States in the nineteenth century, the Caddo people was supposedly saddled by a treaty with the United States, which relinquished approximately one million Caddo acres. In exchange, the Caddo were to move into the Mexican province of Texas within one year from the announcement of the treaty on July 1, 1835. There is no conclusive evidence that such a treaty ever existed. The oral history held by the Hasinai indicates that the Caddo never made such a one-sided agreement with the United States government.

The Caddo were then caught in the violence of the Texas revolution. The Natchitoche divided. A part went among the Choctaw and a part went into Texas to join the Hasinai. A second divisioning took place, with a portion of the Natchitoche moving farther south into Chihuahua under the leadership of Mon-won. They were forced back into Texas to join the Hasinai at Big Arbor after another outbreak of smallpox.[4] Although a treaty was reportedly drawn up there between the United States and the Caddo Confederacy in 1805, no copy could be found by the 1830s. Anglo-American intruders demanded to have the Caddo lands. The last of the Caddo were driven out of Louisiana in 1840.[5]

In 1843, the Hasinai and associated tribes concluded an agreement with the Republic of Texas. The Treaty of Bird's Fort was signed September 19, 1843, on the Trinity River. This was a peace treaty rather than one of cession of additional land.[6] Bintah, *cah-de,* spoke at the first council:

> Our women and children will now be without fear; the road is cleared, for them to travel without danger. I believe that what you have told me is truth, and that from this time henceforth we are friends.[7]

After Texas statehood in 1845, the United States again took control of Indian-white relationships. The Hasinai were removed to the Brazos Reserve near Fort Belknap. The first planting of corn there was killed by grasshoppers. The second was destroyed by drought. The hunting was poor, for game had suffered overkill by the whites and by the Comanches. The cycle was repeated for three years.[8]

In time, the Hasinai agreed to move to Indian Territory. This exodus was completed on August 8, 1859.[9] The Federal Indian Agent for the Hasinai and other tribes, Robert S. Neighbors, wrote: "I have this day crossed all of the Indians out of the heathen land of 'Texas' and am now 'out of the land of the Philistines.'" Neighbors, who later returned to Texas only to be shot in the back and killed,[10] was held in high esteem by the Hasinai because he aided them at a time of terrible need. In gratitude, the Hasinai continue to travel to Fort Belknap each year to honor Neighbors at a graveside ceremony.

The move into Indian Territory was complicated by the American Civil War. Just as the revolution of the Texas Province against Mexican authority worked an extreme hardship upon the Hasinai, the rebellion of the southern states against U.S. authority disrupted ordinary life.[11] Hasinai agricultural and ranching activities flourished as they had in the past. The inner discipline of the Hasinai in planning and maintaining a civilized existence made them a model for the U.S. government to try to impose upon plains tribes. However, the Hasinai culture was as foreign to the Kiowas and Comanches as were Anglo-American ways of thinking. These tribes did not think of themselves as agricultural.[12] The Hasinai had their doubts about the U.S. "peace policy" of Ulysses S. Grant's administration. The attack of the Kiowas and the Comanches against the Wichita Agency in 1874 did not settle their doubts. The deaths of leaders such as José María and Guadelupe made the Reconstruction Period more difficult.[13]

As pressure increased to take Indian Territory lands for increased Anglo-American settlement, the Hasinai fell into line with the hegemony of the U.S. government. The Dawes Act, passed in 1887, began the process by which the Caddo would lose most of the land they held in common. In 1888, Whitebread, the Hasinai *cah-de,* enjoined the president of the United States to remember those who remained at peace:

> We, the affiliated bands made war on no one, and lived as best we could during the Civil War among the white people. After the war, and after the Comanches, Apaches, and Kiowas had made war upon the white people, a treaty was made with them, and our country, the home and country of the Wichitas and affiliated bands, because of their peaceful lives and friendship to the white man, and through their ignorance were not consulted, and have been ignored and stuck away in a corner and allowed to exist by sufferance.[14]

In 1902, some land was allotted to the Caddo people and the remainder was ceded to the U.S. government and its citizens as a part of its efforts to give them a new chance in the southwest.[15]

In the twentieth century, the Hasinai government continued but was restricted in its scope of work by constant interference in the lives of the people by U.S. officials. In 1938 a measure of home rule was provided through the terms of Oklahoma Indian Welfare Act and its acceptance by the enrolled Caddo voters.[16] An elected government was agreed upon and it worked to try to include both internal and external direction of Caddo affairs until the early years of the 1970s. After a disputed election in 1973, the Hasinai internal government went its own way, apart from the interchange with the government of the United States still carried on by the elected Caddo Council. In 1976 a completely new constitution was ratified and put into effect among the Caddo.[17]

Given the forces of change and technology arrayed against it, the Hasinai confederacy reached the limits of its expansion at some time prior to the fifteenth century. Throughout the modern period, the Hasinai found it impossible to maintain a position of leadership in the southwest. With the tremendous impact of disease brought on by contact with European colonists, the Hasinai began to experience reduced returns in agricultural and craft production. Problems in the nineteenth century compounded this situation. Dependence on goods produced outside the Hasinai world brought on increasing fiscal crisis. By the early nineteenth century, differences in the rate of growth brought about a decisive redistribution of power. Other tribes were finding varying degrees of the same type of power shift. Despite the tremendous hardships imposed by the United States, the resulting imposition of power has maintained a relative peace in the region for the past one hundred years.

NINE

Cherokee Dance

HEALTH

The Cherokee dance or *kay-ka-hie-oa-shun* is sometimes called the vine dance. It is started with only the women. The lead dancer is nearly always the same woman. Usually the first few dancers come forward, standing in front of the singers on the west side of the dance ground. The leader takes the line of dancers, who are holding hands, in a winding, unpredictable course. They dance a serpentine course around the dance area and even outside it. The line moves about, coiling, and then straightening out again. Men and children gradually join the dancers. On a cue from the drum, the line of dancers changes hands. The leaders can end the dance by taking a drum stick and pounding the drum. Sometimes the line coils so tightly the dancers can no longer move. Then they cease dancing.

In the Hasinai language, the literal translation of *ha-yah'-noh* or human is "where the soul abides." All conceptions of life and health are built upon that principle. As one lives, one is released from this existence one "lifeline" at a time. In all, everyone is "hooked" in life at four places. As life proceeds, the "hooks" or "lifelines" come loose—in childhood, in adolescence, in middle age, and in old age. When the last "hook" comes off, the person is free to pass away from this material existence. There is no term in the Hasinai language for "death" (human). The "lifelines" are a means through which existence on earth may be measured, so that a person is prepared for the changes that are inevitable.

In the Hasinai understanding of the wholeness of existence, there are no reasons to separate what in English are termed "life" and "death." These are not, in truth, polar opposites. The polarity of West European thought has been influenced heavily by the classical Greek logic, which emphasizes either/or considerations. From the Hasinai perspective the spiritual being continues on its path with the unending multiformity of existence.

This is not to say that fear and superstition do not play a role in health care. Throughout the history of the people, some persons have attempted to command the spiritual forces, but this is a perversion of Hasinai understanding of the cosmos. Forms of witchcraft have been practiced, just as in every society on earth. However, this is the exception rather than the rule.

Illness in a person is treated in a variety of ways. Persons are considered in the environment in which they live in community with those who are closest to them. Normally the room of the sick person is smoked with cedar. In many cases, the person is given a sweat bath. Herbs are used for a variety of reasons, according to the observed need. These have been collected and stored by a knowledgeable person. The herbs or medicines are replaced, at the point where they are gathered, by a gift of tobacco. Among the most common herbs are:

1. sage–used as a tea made from the leaves, sweetened with honey, used for coughs.
2. dogwood–used as a tonic, stimulant, antiseptic, and astringent. The bark of the root or smaller branches is usually dried and made into a powder. It is boiled in water and used for a number of complaints and fever.
3. persimmon–used as an astringent. The bark of the tree and the root used with honey is good for a sore throat. It is used also as a wash or bath for a wound.
4. alumroot–used as an astringent. The root of this small grayish colored plant is useful for bowel problems.
5. peppermint–found in wet lands. Its tea is used in the case of stomach aches.
6. southern yaupon–the leaves of the yaupon, a type of holly, make a pleasant tea, which increases the flow of urine.

In much of the history of the Hasinai, the mescal bean was used extensively in medicine. A whole school of healers grew up around this type of medicine. But just prior to the beginning of the First World War, these practices came to an end. It was felt that medicine using mescal would be abused increasingly in the future. Caddo society no longer practices this traditional form of healing.

When a new philosophy or outlook is being introduced, it is normal for old ways of life to be debunked. This happened when the Spanish missionaries first reached the Hasinai people. The missionaries sought to break the Hasinai faith in their traditional forms of health care. This task was easier with the introduction of disease to which the Hasinai did not have any resistance. Most of the writings of the Spanish missionaries are derogatory. However, Fray Juan Augustín de Morfi admitted in his chronicle:

> One must concede that, in spite of so much error and extravagance, they do sometimes succeed in very singular cures because the land has an abundance of medical herbs, and, knowing many of them, they probably apply them with skill, especially in the healing of wounds, in which they have the greatest practice.[1]

In other words, the Hasinai could work effectively with the diseases and wounds with which they were familiar. The diseases brought by the Europeans were caused by totally different contagions. They were unprepared for these, such as measles, smallpox, and influenza, which suddenly upset the balance of life as the Hasinai knew it.

Now as then, in a person's lifetime the "hooks" are released and may on occasion be rejoined. Then at another time and place the "hook" is released once again. When the last "hook" releases the soul to continue its journey, the traditional designs that are placed on a person's face allow him or her to be recognized by those who have gone on before. This is a difficult concept to explain, but the features of the body continue after the material body has passed away. Although the Hasinai no longer use the elaborate designs and colors, there is still the practice of preparation for "when I go." Ear lobes are painted red, as are the part in the hair and the cheeks of the deceased before the spirit passes away, six days after the body ceases to function. Dinner is prepared on the sixth day to celebrate the soul's leaving the earth. The person is there for the dinner. At that time, those who are left on earth release them to go on. Memorial dinners are then held annually for the following three years.

At the time of burial, the body of the person is dressed by close relatives or friends. The individual who dresses the body talks to the spirit throughout the process. The person that does the honors also talks to the body. They request help to carry on after the person has gone. Then prayers are made to *Ah-ah-ha'-yo* for encouragement. The body is dressed in new traditional clothes. In all cases, the moccasins are split so that when the person comes to the "river," which divides this life from the next, the slits allow the water to flow through to keep the person from drowning.

On the sixth day, the family goes to a stream of fresh running water. There they bathe to cleanse themselves of the spirit. They take tobacco with them. Each person bathes in tobacco before bathing in the water. They begin by facing east. They blow tobacco in each direction, ending with straight up. The remaining loose tobacco is then allowed to fall back on each person's head. The releasing rite continues at the graveside. Water is placed there for everyone present. They all wash their face and hands. In turn, each person throws a handful of dirt into the grave. Personal objects are buried with the person to protect the soul on the continued journey. The grave itself is aligned with the path of the sun. The head of the grave is on the west, so that the body is facing the rising sun.

The reason why the Hasinai wait six days for the dinner for the departed person is connected with the six days of creation. Francis Williams, a Hasinai from Oklahoma, related that during the early period, as the Hasinai emerged from the earth, they saw two figures on the surface—a *ta-sha* or wolf and an evil figure with a pair of horns and a tail, sometimes identified as *Tsa-kee'-yooh.* The *ta-sha* protected the Hasinai at their emergence. Thus, the word *ta-sha* came also to mean friend or ally. During this early period, everything was easy. Hunting was no problem and crops posed little difficulty. In time the people became wasteful. But this was ultimately reversed. This earliest time on earth is closely associated with the six days.[2]

During the six days, the people first fast and then eat in a prescribed manner. The fast lasts for three days. On the fourth day, the family eats *kish'-wa,* the corn dish. On the night of the first day, the body is prepared. The main dinner is prepared on the sixth day. During preparation, nothing is tasted by the cooks. Small portions of each prepared dish are taken from the whole of what is being prepared and burned. Then all who are present eat their portions. This same pattern is carried out for each of the annual memorial dinners. These acts collectively constitute the release of the person by those who remain.[3]

The influx of diseases transported to the Americas in the modern period overwhelmed the medical knowledge of the Hasinai practitioners. The smallpox epidemics were devastating to Hasinai civilization, as was the influx of influenza and other diseases where no resistance had been built up over the centuries. Health among the Hasinai is still a community concern rather than something pertaining only to the isolated individual affected. The lifelines of existence provide an understanding of health that is ordered. Contact with European colonists strained this balanced perspective to its limits. The extreme concern with death by the Anglo-American population in the twentieth century has confused matters even further. Yet even presently, where the Hasinai community is present, life and health concerns can be brought back into a balanced frame of reference.

TEN

Bell Dance

LANGUAGE

The bell dance or *ka-ke-chun-e-shin* is thought to be one of the oldest dances of the Hasinai. It is normally one of the last dances of the night. To start the dance, a few men form a line at the east edge of the dance area. The leader holds a leather strap with large bells attached. The lead singer starts shaking the large bells. (Interestingly, handmade bells have been found in many of the burial mounds in the southwest, including Spiro Mound.) All of the men start singing, "*Yo Ha-see-ney'.*" This phrase is repeated ten times slowly. The dancers start their movement to their left in a line, holding hands.

As the men start to dance, other men and the women rapidly join the line of dancers. The women move in between the men and begin to hold hands. The long line or lines move around the dance ground in a clockwise pattern starting in the west. If there are many dancers, two parallel lines are formed with a leader for each line. More than a dozen songs are normally sung to complete the cycle. The pattern of the dance is a winding one. The line is coiled in on itself during one song and then unwound during the next song. This is repeated throughout the dance sequence. Many of the dancers sing along with the leader.

The relationships of language to experience are essential to understanding Hasinai history and society. The added insights provided by the Hasinai words for objects and actions offer a glimpse into the richness that characterizes their world. The traditional essence of the people is passed from generation to generation through language as well as through genetic ties. Any translation of that connection into another language loses some of the insights and precisions of the Hasinai people. Some of the most important studies of the language have been made by Sadie Bedoka, a Hasinai. Her notes, which resulted from her work with the language with Wallace L. Chafe, provide some of the most reliable perspectives on the Hasinai language. It is important to compare her work and the understanding of other native speakers with the published materials of Professor Chafe as found in his book *The Caddoan, Iroquoian, and Siouan Languages,* and his article "Caddoan."[1]

The most important resources of the Hasinai language are the oral documents used in ceremonial affairs. The traditional history of the Hasinai is related in the songs of two dances – the drum dance and the turkey dance. The drum dance records the origins and early migrations of the Hasinai. The turkey dance relates the specific events that constitute the classic and modern history of the Hasinai. Contained in the songs of the turkey dance are stories of military engagements with other peoples such as the Chickasaw and the Osage, as well as the record of natural phenomena that have affected the lives of the Hasinai, such as the overnight creation of Caddo Lake. The words of each song remain the same, but new songs may be added to document new events. Important additions are added to the structure of the overall song sequence.

Two versions of Hasinai are used in Oklahoma – the common speech, which is also the language of the ceremonial songs, and the prayer language. The first of the two is the subject of all research. The latter is considered the province of select Caddo men who possess the discipline to have access to this special knowledge.

The turkey dance, the bell dance, and the drum dance, among other songs, have been recorded and stored in the collections of the Hasinai Cultural Center and the Duke Oral History Collection of the Western History Manuscripts Collection of the University of Oklahoma. Commercial recordings have been made of some of the most familiar of the Hasinai songs. The most easily accessible recording is "Songs of the Caddo," in two tapes distributed by Canyon Records. In the past, the principal means of learning the language of the songs was through repetition in the home and at the ceremonial ground. Tape recordings now play a larger role in teaching the songs, but this is not true of the prayer language. The prayer language is spoken by few and only in sacred petition.

Language study by the Hasinai themselves has been limited largely to recording songs and stories. From these records, word lists have emerged, which have begun to provide a solid base of investigation of the structure of the language. Hasinai language instruction outside the home began in a systematic way only in the 1970s. Courses of instruction in Hasinai have been conducted at the Fort Cobb Vocational and Technical School and at the Caddo Tribal Complex in the 1985–1986 academic year. Some instruction materials have been developed and reproduced. No manuscripts in Hasinai were recorded before the twentieth century. Tribal leadership has attempted to offer formal language instruction through the tribal organization and area schools.

Most Hasinai spoke more than one language. Many in recent times in Oklahoma also spoke Delaware, or Kickapoo, or Kiowa. In an earlier period, the Hasinai could communicate with the other tribes in eastern Texas, including those that spoke Tonkawa or Atakapa. The Spanish missionary Fray Morfi wrote in the seventeenth century:

> But all of them [east Texas Indians] find it convenient to use another kind of language, in which it is not necessary to use the tongue, and that is the sign language with which they are exceedingly clever. They send ambassadors to one another and they are days at a time in conversation treating on subjects of lasting importance, explaining and making each other understand the most hidden thoughts, without need of words.[2]

In the twentieth century, English has become the principal means of intertribal communication.

As in many other American Indian languages, Caddoan verbal forms are complex. Nominal elements are found in a variety of ways in verbal forms and in independent forms. In the verb, nominal elements designate aspects of person, case, and number, and describe the subject. For example, in some cases the number of the subject is reflected in the surface structure of the verb. Chafe noted that the relative order of all parts of the surface structure verb are:

1	2	3	4	5	6
person case	dual	nonsingular object	preverb	plural animate	verb proper

In nearly all cases, the verb is inflected in terms of some particular tense or aspect. The speaker indicates the personal relationship to what is being said. If the speaker is repeating information gained from another source rather than firsthand experience, this can be made clear with the prefix *kan*. Assessment of the information may be indicated by prefixes such as *tak*, which parallels the idea of "possibly," or *tuk*, which approximates the idea of "probably." A negative assessment of the validity of a statement is usually expressed by the prefix *was*. There are approximately one hundred prefixes that may precede the person-case prefixes.[3]

One of the best indications of the logic of Hasinai thought is found in the language of mathematics. The Hasinai construction of the numerical progression is:

wis'-tsi = one
bit = two
da-ho' = three
he-wih' = four
dec'-see-kun = five
dun'-key = six
bit'-see-kuh = seven
da-ho'-see-kuh = eight
he-wih'-see-kuh = nine
bi-nay'-uh = ten

Then the progression continues with prefixes:

bi-nay'-uh-hi-yo-wis-tsi = eleven
bi-nay'-uh-hi-yo-bit = twelve

Progressing by units of ten:

bi-nay'-ah-bit = twenty
bi-nay'-ah-bit-hi-yo-wis'-tsi = twenty-one
bi-nay'-ah-da-ho' = thirty
bi-nay'-ah-da-ho'-hi-yo-wis'-tsi = thirty-one
bi-nay'-ah-he-wih' = forty
bi-nay'-ah-he-wih'-hi-yo-wis'-tsi = forty-one
bi-nay'-ah-dec'-see-kun = fifty
bi-nay'-ah-dun'-key = sixty
bi-nay'-ah-dun'-key-hi-yo-wis'-tsi = sixty-one
bi-nay'-ah-bit-see-kuh = seventy

bi-nay'-ah-da-ho'-see-kuh = eighty
bi-nay'-ah-he-wih'-see-kuh = ninety

The logical progression then continues:

wis-tsi-hi-ya-shu = one hundred
wis-tsi-hi-ya-shu-bi-nay-ah-hi-yo-wis-tsi = one hundred eleven
wis-tsi-hi-ya-shu-bi-nay-ah-bit = one hundred twenty
bit-hi-ya-shu = two hundred
wis'-tsi-hu-nis'-tee = one thousand

Games provide a means to combine the Hasinai logic of language and numbers in enjoyable combination. One of the most popular games is the hand game or *ca-kee-see-kut'-cha.* There are many songs associated with the game. The singers with the drum are seated at the end of two lines of players, facing one another. The scorekeepers with the tally sticks are placed at the opposite end of the two lines of players. The object of the game is for a "guesser" to pick which hand the bead or bone piece is concealed in. Rapid motion of the hands and arms of the person on the team holding the button is done in time with the fast drum and song to make the guessing process more difficult. Usually the two opposing teams have an equal number of players. The play goes up and down the line, hiding and guessing. When a team reaches a given score, it wins. Then a victory dance is performed, before the next game. Logic, odds, strategy, and intuition all play an important role in the hand game.

Among the tribes of the Caddo confederacy, most terms were mutually intelligible. However, there were greater differences in word form and substance in conversing with other Caddo tribes in the two other groupings on the Red River—the Natchitoche and the Kadohadacho:

Hasinai	*Natchitoche*	*Kadohadacho*	*English*
bah′-tah′	wa-st′n	ba′-ta	fish
cooh′-whooh	ko-ho′s	ko′-ho	alligator
do′-ooh	do′	doe′	rabbit
nee′-cooh	i′-tok	ni′-ki-o	fire
note′-tsi	na′m-tsi	na′-ot-si	bear

Hasinai	*Natchitoche*	*Kadohadacho*	*English*
tah′-nah-ha	ta′-na	ta′-na-ha	buffalo
tah′-ooh	tc-lao′k	tiao′x	beaver
wah′-dooh′	ma-do′	wa-do	wildcat
wah-dut	ma′-dat	wa′-dat	dirt

Some other words are pronounced essentially the same in each of the dialects:

bit′-teh (cedar)
cah-pah′-tsi cah-ko′-ah (chicken hawk)
dah (deer)
e-yah-wut-see (antelope)
kun′ (duck)
nah-ti-dooh (south)
sah-ha′ (walnut)
ta′-sha (wolf)
tsa-tah′-win (possum)
tsah-toch (rat)

The Hasinai language expresses reality in independence of human experience. In other words, human experience is related in all things to extrahuman reality, which is unbound, undifferentiated, and synchronic. In all Hasinai expression, there is a balance in time and space relationships. The natural order of expression finds a balance between the collective and the singular. One is comfortable in the broad range of individual effort within the collective whole. To emphasize one over the other is to divorce oneself from reality. When the Hasinai language is spoken, it offers insights into life in the American southwest.

ELEVEN

Morning Dance

CONTEMPORARY AFFAIRS

The morning dance customarily ends a night of dancing. It cannot be done, however, unless the dancing has continued uninterrupted throughout the entire night. As the singers walk very slowly around the arena with the drum, the dancers gather on one or both sides of them. They face the drum with their arms linked at the elbows. There is much freedom of movement by one person, or a couple, or a small group. Each person or group moves in a light, nearly trotting, step. They move toward the drum, then away from it, until a cue from the singers indicates another change in direction. This brings about a smooth flow to and from the drum. There are many songs. When the usual series of songs is completed, any one of the several singers may start another exuberant or humorous song as the dance continues until the first light of the sun. At dawn, the dance is concluded and all dancers express their respect for the others present, then leave the dance area.

The Hasinai work in concert with the other peoples through the Caddo Tribe of Oklahoma. It is a federally recognized entity—the most convenient one with which to respond to the civil needs of the people. The Caddo tribal complex is located on thirty-seven acres of tribal controlled land that also contains the dance ground. It is about seven miles north of Gracemont in Caddo County. The new office center was financed by a $254,000 grant from the United States government. In these offices, tribal dealings with the federal government are conducted. Elected tribal chairpersons have led the council or executive committee of the chartered tribal entity to take advantage of several federal programs for the benefit of the

Caddo people. In addition to the health and housing programs of the late 1960s and early 1970s, the Caddo tribe has taken grants for senior citizens' programs, work-training programs, grants to supplement the payment of utility bills, and organizational purposes. As a former Caddo tribal administrator, Gayle Cussen Satepauhoodle, stated: "The federal grant money is marvelous and we appreciate it so much. But there may come a time when the public will not be so generous. We don't want to depend on anybody. We want to be self-sufficient."[1]

To this goal of self-sufficiency, the Caddo *nit-tso-sah-dos-cha-ah* or tribal chairpersons from Melford Williams to Hubert Halfmoon have sought means to bring small industry to the area. Normally, plans intend that the chartered tribal entity would own the corporate interests. However, planning is widening to involve various independent corporate enterprises to locate on tribal properties. It is also planned that a clinic could be established in this rural area, so that the sick and injured would not have to be taken to the Indian Service hospital in Lawton for treatment. A senior citizens' center is already in place. Each *nit-tso-sah-dos-cha-ah*, when possible, has built upon the advantages passed by the previous one. But all too often changes in administration in Washington, D.C., have changed working relationships, so that they have become very difficult.

Since Williams stepped down from the office, the *nit-tso-sah-dos-cha-ah* has been Harry Guy, Doyle Edge, Calvin Toho, Mary Pat Francis, Henry Shemayme, and Hubert Halfmoon (elected in 1986). The election of the first woman to the position, Pat Francis, brought to the surface an issue surrounding the internal and external functions of tribal leadership. The role of the *nit-tso-sah-dos-cha-ah* was defined by the Oklahoma Indian Welfare Act of 1936, as well as by the subsequent Caddo Tribal Constitution and Charter of 1938. The character of the position was determined externally by the United States government. It has little tradition built up around it, except where it is confused with the role of the *cah-de*. With the election of the first woman *nit-tso-sah-dos-cha-ah*, confusion escalated to consternation. Elected tribal government was brought to a standstill in the spring of 1983 for this very reason. In this crisis, the differences between the *nit-tso-sah-dos-cha-ah* and

George and Stella Beaver.

From left: Alice Timmons, director of the Phillips Collection; Oscar Jacobson, art professor at the University of Oklahoma; and Vynola Newkumet, head of the OU Music Library.

Vynola Newkumet digging a small hole for tobacco at Robert Neighbors's grave, 1981.

Singers and dancers at the turkey dance, Binger, Oklahoma, 1971.

Melford Williams, Caddo tribal chairman, 1967–71.

T. C. Canon, Caddo-Kiowa artist.

Donnie Frank, tribal chairperson, 1988.

the *cah-de* are all too real. First, the former is an elective position open to enrolled members of the tribe above the age of twenty-one irrespective of sex, whereas the latter is a male, hereditary position bound up with the long history of the confederacy. Secondly, the primary function of the elected chairperson's role is to act as intermediary for the people with the U.S. government. The *cah-de* retains the role of seeing to it that all factions within the confederacy have the opportunity to have a voice in decisions that affect the whole.

Although men and women are both to have opportunities to function in meaningful ways, they are not to participate in exactly the same ways. The traditional way calls for complementary roles. The Hasinai conceive of a hierarchy of power and responsibility in which each person does the duty assigned to him or her. Traditional government is not a meeting of persons on the same level. Each voice is weighted according to tradition. Government is an obligation by those born to the role and for the benefit of all. Obedience without discussion of "whys and wherefores" is a duty. In the traditional sense, the Hasinai remain a community led by the enlightened, the responsible, and the successful. Its solidarity is hierarchical in nature. Its foundation is found in a social structure that is ancient and enduring.

The Hasinai have gone forward with the technological changes introduced through West European colonialism. They are a people who, in the past and probably in the future, identify their interests with those of faraway peoples—peoples from outside the traditional circle of their own loyalties and political responsibilities.

In efforts to retain their identity in this increasingly confused environment, new forms have been sought to make this task more manageable. One important step was the creation of the Whitebead Hasinai Cultural Center in 1975. Its stated purposes include:

1. The perpetuation of Caddo culture;
2. The preservation of Caddo lands, customs, music, dances, crafts, and traditions;
3. The encouragement of youth to maintain a strong interest in tribal values and traditions;

4. The evaluation of the best aspects of bicultural life;
5. The study of the Caddo language, dances, and history.[2]

The original trustees included Reuben Whitebead of Hinton; Winona M. Williams of Fort Cobb; Ellen Williams of Lookeba; and Justine Whitebead of Binger. Its membership understood the traditional hierarchy of judgment. The corporate system became a means of dealing with change–to perpetuate a value system within a hostile environment.

When a people not only fashions rules for society far in excess of individual personal need, but keeps them over the centuries, it is a sign of an advanced civilization. With the Hasinai sense of administration developed a social pattern, a sense of proportion in guiding human affairs in response to the environment of the American southwest.

In the period since World War II, tension between the traditional Hasinai sense of governance and the system imposed as a result of New Deal reforms of the late 1930s have come into increasing conflict. At this juncture, the Hasinai are still a part of the federal system of the United States through the Caddo Tribe of Oklahoma. But traditional values are becoming more difficult to relate to the next generation. As technology allows greater freedom of movement, the community is more difficult to maintain.

During the same period, the pursuit of the identification of the territory of the Caddo Tribe of Oklahoma before the Indian Claims Commission has brought a renewed sense of understanding to many tribal members. Ethnohistorical research has attempted to find concrete evidence of the limits of the land occupied by the ancestors of the Hasinai and the other tribes of the Caddo confederacy in Texas, Louisiana, Arkansas, and Oklahoma. Written accounts of the Caddo peoples by colonial Europeans and material evidence from archeological fieldwork provided much of the evidence that was recognized by the Indian Claims Commission. Language study and tradition provided additional evidence. Archeologists from the four-state region have consulted with one another on an annual basis to correlate their information. The attempt to assemble and correlate historical documents from French, Spanish, Mexican, and American archives began in the 1980s. These efforts have inspired many Hasinai to cooperate with this traditional work of history to ensure balance in addition to academic objectivity. The Hasinai tradition is a living tradition.

TWELVE

Turkey Dance

HISTORICAL PERSPECTIVES

The *nuh'-ka-oa-shun* or turkey dance stands alone among the Hasinai dances. It relates, within the structure of the songs and dance, the stream of events that define the history of the Hasinai people. Unlike the other Caddo dances, it is done by women only and is performed in the afternoon. The *nuh'-ka-oa-shun* used to be danced in the early afternoon, usually between two and five o'clock. In more recent years, it has been danced just before sunset.

For this dance, the *kai-a-cooh* or drum is placed in the center of the *ko-na-cha-ka-wa-ah-so* or dance ground. The drum is always treated with respect. All Hasinai drums have flint or charcoal (from a fire started with flint) inside them. This tradition looks back to the time of the emergence into the present world. The singers sit around the drum. They begin by calling the turkey dancers. The first of seven songs in this sequence says: "Come, you turkeys," as the women dancers begin to arrive in the ring. The women begin to do a straight dance step in a circle, dancing on the balls of their feet. The song continues, "kick, kick" the dirt. The second song repeats the message of the first, but in Haish, a dialect that is now extinct. The third song is in the Neche dialect and refers to the growing number of dancers. The fourth song then sings out: "Come on, you Hainais," in that dialect. The next song says: "Come on, Yona." It continues with indications that dancers are there in the *ko-na-cha-ka-wa-ah-so* and are proceeding to dance. The sixth and seventh songs are in the Kechai dialect, reinforcing the themes of the fourth and fifth songs.

By the end of this first segment of songs, the dance ground is filled with the color and movement of the women in their traditional dress. The turkey dancers wear beautiful clothing of every color. This includes a one-piece dress, usually calico, with long sleeves. They also have aprons that are tied at the waist. In addition to these, their most distinctive feature is the *dush-tooh* tied to their hair braid. It is decorated with ribbon pendants and streamers, with shell or small round mirrors attached. In addition, the women carry shawls and feather fans.

The second series of songs is the longest. The women in single file follow the leading dancer, imitating a turkey's gait, darting each foot forward in turn, then quickly drawing it back before planting it on the ground. The feet alternate in rapid succession.

During this phase, the songs relate the events of the Hasinai past. Many of these songs are of military engagements with the Kiowa, the Choctaw, the Apache, and the Osage. Many of them are no longer sung, out of respect for friends among the Kiowa, the Osage, and others. All the historical songs are sung in this portion while the dancers are still dancing around the singers.

Some of the songs make reference to events long before the transfers to Oklahoma. The most notable example relates the eyewitness version of two brothers during the creation of Caddo or Sodo Lake, on the Louisiana-Texas border. It begins with the people dancing in the evening. More than one village was present during the night's dancing. As the dancers continued, the water began to rise. The two brothers went to higher ground because they were worried about the rising water. But the dancers in the valley continued on without distraction. The older of the two brothers called out: "Let's go to higher ground—we might all drown." But the others went on dancing despite his effort. The brothers looked to the east and saw a ridge of land moving around as if it were a great snake. This undulating form was holding back the water. Others came and saw the snakelike movement, while the lake formed upstream. The dancers were no longer above the surface of the water. They were lost to the lake, only to reappear as fantastic creatures. The dawn allowed those people who had gone to high ground to see the natural levee and the lake that had formed behind it.

New events may be added to the traditional history, by any of the dancers. One of them dances over to the drummers and grabs the drumsticks of one of the singers. The dancer than relates the event and the singers make up a song that is the key to recalling the event. It may be sung that one time or incorporated into the pattern of songs of the people's history. In this way, new events are keyed again and again for subsequent generations.

The origin of the dance, in and of itself, is lost to human memory. The following story is most frequently told in reference to the beginnings of this dance among the Hasinai. A young warrior was hunting in the woods one day, when he heard beautiful songs. Tracing the sound to its source, he discovered a number of turkey hens dancing around a group of gobblers. He watched and listened until he had fixed the dance in his memory. After he returned to his village, he related what he had learned. The villagers began to use it and it became a fundament of Hasinai historiography. Others believe that Hasinai civilization was closely related to the turkey and its roosts, which served as an important criterion for the location of village life.

During the third phase of the dance, the women spread out to the edge of the *ko-na-cha-ka-wa-ah-sa,* then return to its center. This is repeated. During these songs, the women keep their feet together and skip or hop. At the same time, they turn their bodies from left to right and then right to left. In both the second and third phases, the women look to the leading dancer for the keys in the dance sequence.

The lead dancer is responsible for presenting the singers with tobacco. She also wears bells around her ankles. When she becomes too old to continue to dance this arduous dance, she gives a speech indicating that she is stepping aside. It is sad in some ways, but also a time of joy as a new leader is made known. She is usually related in some way to the previous lead dancer. Many gifts are lavished upon the new lead dancer by the retiring dancer.

The last segment of the sequence is begun as the women start with a toe-heel left then a toe-heel right step in a circle. After a short while each woman dancer picks a male partner from among those sitting around the circumference of the dance area. Each man dances backward facing his partner. On musical cue the men whoop and change positions with the female partners. She is then dancing backward. The same reversals are repeated at the end of each song. If a man chooses not to dance, he must give an article of clothing to the woman, such as a hat or scarf. The woman dances with this piece of clothing. At the end of the dance, the man must pay some sort of token to retrieve his article of clothing. In this segment, a woman never dances with a close relative. This portion of the dance is called the *wa-hu.*

This dance and the drum dance stand at the very heart of Hasinai civilization. The history of the Hasinai is linked with the turkey dance.[1]

The Hasinai are well aware of the major differences among the peoples of the Americas. There are lingering tales of travel by Hasinai men to the tundra regions of the north and to the Andes Mountains in the south. Legends of Mayan boats crossing the Gulf of Mexico for purposes of trade and colonization are a part of the same heritage. Long before European contacts of the modern period, the Hasinai had a solid understanding of the lands of the Americas, centering in the American southwest. Questions on the origins of human beings in the Americas and the dawn of civilization have found no answers that have won universal consensus of thought among the people involved. Hasinai tradition places the origin of the Caddo peoples in this hemisphere.

West European and Anglo-American scholars have perhaps been too ready to acclaim the youth of the "New World." The Pleistocene period witnessed successive advances of ice sheets from the north over large areas of Europe, Asia, and North America. It also was the age that witnessed the advent of the human species. It has been theorized outside Hasinai circles that American Indian peoples came from Asia to the Americas at a relatively late period. Yet modern studies of blood groups suggest no simple or close affinity between Native Americans and Asian racial stocks.[2]

According to Hasinai tradition, when the first human beings came into the present world, they carried two types of seeds with them–corn or maize and pumpkin. The Hasinai still have these varieties of plants; they brought them with them to Oklahoma. There are many studies on corn or maize. Fossil pollen grains of maize have been found below the present site of Mexico City dating back approximately eighty thousand years. Two varieties of early corn found in Mexico are Nat-Tel and Chapalote. The latter variety has also been found in abundance in early Caddoan sites. This base for agricultural surpluses allowed for the development of large villages and ceremonial centers in the Hasinai region.[3] It has been suggested that a new way of life emerged there, based on agronomy and the use of a new, more adaptable variety of corn. William H. Sears wrote: "Certainly the standards set in the Caddoan area at this time became effective because very shortly we see that Caddoan culture, ceremonial centers, and pottery proliferate."[4]

Hasinai civilization is one among many scattered over space and time. Its culture is a collection of inherited characteristics and phenomena associated with the American southwest. Its influence has waxed and waned in response to changing situations.

Hasinai civilization has a representative center in the Caddo Tribal Complex north of Anadarko and Gracemont in Oklahoma. This small complex contains the ceremonial dance ground, the offices of the elected tribal council, the Caddo Cultural Center, the "Community House," as well as individual cabins. It is a tribal center in the traditional American Indian sense. The history of the Hasinai is found in essence in the turkey dance, which is danced on the complex dance ground. The complex offers the general public a means of assimilating beliefs and action patterns from the past. Caught up in this are conceptions of right order for society as well as standards of conduct in private and public life.

Human action has a history behind it. Colonial elements in the population of the Americas today can benefit from the Indian heritage of this land. It would be short-sighted to ignore the rich Caddo culture that has learned to be itself and to live as an integrated part of creation.

Ah-ah ha-ah-hut kit-see-yah-ah.[5]

GLOSSARY

HASINAI/ENGLISH

A

A′-c-sha *v.* To move closer.

Ah

Ah-ah *n.* Father.
Ah-ah-ha′-yo *n.* God; Father above; Father in heaven.
Ah-ah-e′-may *n.* Older uncle on the male side of the family.
Ah-ah-e-nah *n.* Grandfather on the female side of the family.
Ah-ah hi-u coo-e′-ha *n.* Heaven; "home where God lives." *See* Kee-wut′-hi-u
Ah-ah ti-ti *n.* Younger uncle on the male side of the family.
Ah′-kin *n.* Son.
Ah-hey *n.* Older aunt on the male side of the family.
Ah-hey′-ti-ti *n.* Younger aunt on the male side of the family.
Ah-nah *adj., adv.* Alone. *Ah′-nah tse′-de-ha* (I am going alone); *Ah′-nah tse-wit′-de-ha* (You are going alone).
Ay′-shah *interjection, informal.* Good heavens!

Bah

Bah′ *n.* 1. Projectile; arrow; dart; bullet; 2. Acorns from a black-jack oak.
Bah-caht′-no *n.* Law.
Bah-cha′-dah *n.* Sunflower (wild). *See* Bah′-hun.
Bah-chu′-cah *n., v.* Death; to die (as, an animal died).
Bah′-din *n.* Turtle (water).
Bah-ha′-tse *n.* Lambs-quarters (a plant).
Bah′-ha Sah-sin *n.* Mississippi River.

Bah′-hat-te-no *n.* Red River.
Bah-hey′ *n.* Beans. *See* Dah′-bus.
Bah′-hun *n.* Sunflower (domestic). *See* Bah-cha′-dah.
Bah′-kin-chee *n.* Grandson.
Bah-noo-shah *n., adj.* Green.
Bah-noose′ *n.* Butterfly.
Bah-ooh *n.* Blood.
Bah-she-tah-num′-ba *n.* Dragonfly.
Bah′-tah′ *n.* Fish.
Bah-te-nah′-win *n.* Whirlwind.

Be
Be n. Lice.
Be-nun′-coo n. 1. Light; 2. Kerosene.
Be-tih n. Fear.
Be-yoon′-na-ah n. Hair. *See* Cah-be-yoon′-na.
Beau′-chee *n.* Knee.

Bi
Bish′-tooh *n.* Hat.
Bish′-tsi *n.* Ear.
Bit′-teh *n.* Cedar tree.

Bu
Bun′-cus *n.* Lizard.
Bun′-it *n.* Bird.
Bun′-ooh *n.* Gravey.
Bung-cah-do-ey *n.* Lightning bug.
Bus-cah′-nooh *n.* Gray horse.
But′ *n.* Dance roach.
But′-nen *n.* Button.

Ca
Ca-ah *n.* Brain or mind.
Ca-ah-nah′-ah *n., plural.* Trees. Co-duch′-ah *singular.* tree.
Ca-ha-ne-swah′-cha *n.* Door.
Ca-ha-uh′ *n.* Ghost.
Ca-min *n.* Thunder.

Cah

Cah-ay′-hut *v.* To pass away.
Cah-ah-hun′-ay-you *v.* To laugh.
Cah-ah-nah′-cha *n.* Bone. *See* Nah′-cooh.
Cah-ah-nee-um′-mah *v.* To meet.
Cah-ah-neh′ *v.* To cut. *See* Cah-kee′-cush.
Cah-ah-see-cha′-nee *n., v.* 1. Ghost dance; 2. To hold hands.
Cah-ah-we-dah′-cooh *v.* To attack.
Cah-ah-wish′-nooh-ah *v.* To cough.
Cah-ah-yah′-choot *v.* To tire.
Cah-be-nah′-sah *v., n.* 1. To fight; 2. War.
Cah-be yoon′-na or Cah-be-yoon′-na-ah *n.* Hair. *See* Be-yoon′-na-ah.
Cah-bin-a′-sah *n.* War.
Cah-bish′-nah-ah *n.* Traditional Caddo dress with a large collar.
Cah′-biss *adj.* Speckled.
Cah-bus′-toh *n.* Leaf.
Cah′-but-ooh *n.* Thread.
Cah-ca-yah′-ah *n.* Gopher.
Cah-cah-bah′-tsa *n.* String. *See* Cah-kee-bin′-tsa.
Cah-cah-che′-ah *n.* Cloud.
Cah-cah-cun′-na-ah *n.* Cabbage.
Cah-cah-e′-pah-tah *n.* Flood.
Cah-cah-nay′-dah-wits′-ah *n.* Number.
Cah-cah-say′-day-ah *n.* Arbor.
Cah-cah-wah-nah′-ah *n.* Cigarettes.
Cah-cah-we-ah *n.* Saw.
Cah-cah-yah′ tsa *n.* Ditch.
Cah-can-e′-sah *n.* Lake.
Cah-coo′-its′-sah *n.* Vest.
Cah-dah-cush-nah′-ah *n.* Shell.
Cah-de (*or* cah-di) *n.* Chief; leader.
Cah-de′-soon′-dah *n.* Officer.
Cah-dun′-na *n.* Skin.
Cah-dun′-nooh *n.* Hide; leather.
Cah-dus′-cah *n.* Buckskin horse.
Cah-e-cha′-da-ya *v.* To float.
Cah-e-swe-wah-ho′-kit *n.* Pears.
Cah-e-tsi *n.* Screech owl. *See* Nee-hee.

Cah-e-ush'-ah *n.* Smoke.
Cah'-es-cha'-ah *n.* Day.
Cah-ha-nah'-tsa-ah *n.* Meal of cooked food.
Cah-ha-ne-say'-ah *n.* House.
Cah-ha'-wist *n.* Eye glasses.
Cah-hoat'-in-nuh-nah'-kit *n.* Breeze.
Cah-how-din'-ooh-nah *n.* Electrical storm; lightning.
Cah-hun-mo'-sa *n.* Hill; a natural elevation of the earth's surface.
Cah-kee'-ah-kuh nih-kee-nay'-oh *n.* Woman dance; "standing and singing."
Cah-kee'-ah nee-o' *adj., informal.* Cowardly (I am cowardly).
Cah-kee'-ah-shu'-we *adj., informal.* Brave (I am brave).
Cah-kee'-bin *v.* To hit. *See* Dah'bin.
Cah-kee-bin-ay'-ah *n.* Ribbons. *See* Dush-tooh.
Cah-kee-bin'-tsa *n.* String. *See* Cah-cah-bah'-tsa.
Cah-kee-cah'-cah *v.* To cry. *See* Da-cah'-ah.
Cah-kee-chuh'-ti *n.* Car; automobile.
Cah-kee'-cus-neh *n.* Boil; an inflamed swelling under the skin.
Cah-kee'-cush *v.* To cut. *See* Cah-ah-neh'.
Cah-kee'-de-kee *v.* To sleep.
Cah-key'-dit-ooh *v.* To ride.
Cah-kee-do'-nee *v.* To gather; to collect as in a harvest.
Cah-kee'-dooh *n.* Bite.
Cah-kee-dun'-nay'-ah *n.* Peas.
Cah-kee-hay'-bah *v.* To look.
Cah-kee-hay'-wah-oot *v.* To hunt.
Cah-kee-hun'-nah *v.* To cook.
Cah-kee-hung'-cah-hay *v.* To help. *See* Dah-hung'-cah-hay.
Cah-kee'-keeh *v.* To kill.
Cah-kee'-nee-yooh *v.* To break.
Cah-kee-neh'-oh *v.* To sing.
Cah-kee-no'-noot *v.* To like.
Cah-kee'-nah *v.* To make.
Cah-kee-se-cut'-cha *n.* Handgame.
Cah-kee-te-tsu-kin *v.* To finish.
Cah-kee-tun-che-nee *adj.* Easily seen or understood; clear; not confused.
Cah-kee-us swe-yah-ah *v.* To walk around. *See* Cah-kee-yah-swe'-ah.

Cah-kee-ush-no′-yah *v.* To eat.
Cah-kee-yah-swe′-ah *v.* To walk. *See* Cah-kee-us swe-yah-ah.
Cah-kee-yah′ *v.* To live.
Cah-key′-ah. *v.* To be; exist.
Cah-key-cah′-neeh *v.* To buy; purchase.
Cah-key-cut′-dah-ah *v.* To visit.
Cah-key′-nah *v.* To build; make; create.
Cah-key-we-hah *adj.* Empty.
Cah-kin′-cus-neh *v.* To boil.
Cah-kin′-dah-ah *v.* To find.
Cah-kin-ho′-nee *v.* To move.
Cah-kit-em′-bin *n.* Drum dance; traditionally the first dance of the night; the dance reflects the history of the Caddo people.
Cah-nah-ha *n.* Village headman.
Cah-nah-tswe′-teh n. Needle.
Cah-nay′-ah *v.* To arrange things.
Cah-ne-oot-tsah-ne′-ha *n.* Path.
Cah-noosh′-ta *n.* Metal bowl. *See* Cah-wis.
Cah-o-ah-say′-oo-nah *n.* Mole.
Cah-o-chum′-may *v.* To be bothered.
Cah-o′-dah-ha *n.* Cap.
Cah-o-me-tsa′-see-nine-cooh-ooh *v.* To wonder.
Cah-o′-shun-nee-sah *n.* That dance (specific).
Cah-o′-tsa-a *adj.* Pitiful; poor.
Cah-o′-tsis-nah *n.* Need.
Cah-o′-tsun-ning-coo-oh *n.* Dunce.
Cah′-one-nus-tsi *n.* Goat.
Cah-oo′-tooh *n.* Meat, usually refers to beef. *See* Wah′-cus.
Cah-oo-ko′-yah-hoe′-nen *v.* To answer; echo.
Cah′-ooh *n.* Cotton.
Cah-oot′-nah-way *v.* To ache in one particular area.
Cah-oot′-no′-wih *v.* To ache generally, all over.
Cah-own′-e-kah *v.* To desire.
Cah-pah′-tsi *n.* Chicken.
Cah-pah′-tsi cah-ko′-ah *n.* Chicken hawk.
Cah-peh′ *n.* Coffee.
Cah-put′ *n.* Coat.
Cah′-sah *n.* Mosquito.

Cah-shu *n.* Leg.
Cah′ shuh *n.* Blackbird.
Cah-sooh *n.* Blizzard.
Cah-sue *n.* Icy limbs on trees.
Cah-sun′-ooh *n.* Weed.
Cah-tse *pronoun.* Me; self.
Cah-un *n.* Bottle.
Cah-un′-cah *v.* To burn.
Cah-un′-cah-us *n.* Hot pepper. *See* De′-tooh-tse.
Cah-us cah′-dee *n.* Little plums.
Cah-us′ cah-e-chun′-nah-ah *n.* Big plums.
Cah-us choo′-tooh *n.* Peaches; literally, "hairy fruit."
Cah-us hine′-cooh *n.* Apples.
Cah-wah-sin′-neeh *n.* Shawl.
Cah-we-cha *n.* Cloth.
Cah-wis *n.* Ceramic bowl. *See* Cah-noo′-sah.
Cah′-wist *n.* Eye glasses. *See* Cah-ha′-wist.
Cah-ye-tsi *n.* Neches River.
Cah-yo′-tsi. *n.* Baby.

Cai

Cai′-cooh *n.* Drum. *See* Kai-a-cooh
Cai′-coo-tze *n.* Bells.
Cai-e′ cah-cai′-ah *n.* Flint.

Ch

Cha-ah′ *interjection.* Don't! (prohibition).
Cha-cah-nee-nah *n.* "Place of crying."
Cha-kah-eh′ *n.* Skillet.
Cha-wee *n.* Bow.
Cha′-yah *n.* Terrapin.
Cah-yun′-nah-hum *n.* Floor.
Chah′-dooh *adj.* Alike in looks. *Koo chahdooh pew-dah-ney′-ah* (They look alike).
Chah′-dooh pew-dah-ney′-ah *n.* Identical twins.
Chah-teh′ *v.* To wait; postpone an action.
Cho′-ka-see ti-ti *n.* December.

Cho-oss *n.* Fox.
Choh'-coo-nee *n.* Hummingbird.
Choh'-cah-koot *n.* Currents; water or air moving in a specific direction.
Chu-tooh *n.* Fur.
Chun'-ti-nooh *n.* Tomatoes.
Chun'-de-cooh *n.* Prunes.

Coo

Coo-ah-chun'-ah *n.* Eyes.
Coo-ah-chun'-cah-ah *n.* Face.
Coo'-ah-nah *adj.* Alone. *See* Ah-nah.
Coo-ah-nah-tsu'-nah *n.* Buttock. *See* Coo-ah-yah-do'-sah.
Coo-ah-nee'-yah *n.* Body.
Coo-ah-sue'-ah *n.* Nose; literally, "where the nose is."
Coo-ah-yah-do'-sah *n.* Hip.
Coo-bin-day-nah *adj.* Full. *Coo-bin-day'-nah-hah* (I'm full).
Coo'-cah-cha'-ah *n.* Sky.
Coo-chah-doo pen-dah-ney'-ah *adj.* Common, plain.
Coo-cun-coo *n.* Liver (animal).
Coo-dee'-dah-yut *interjection.* Get away.
Coo-kah-yah-dah'-cha *n.* Spring (water).
Coo-kee-we'-neh-bee' *n.* Fish dance; "going sideways."
Coo'-nah *n.* Doctor of medicine.
Coo-nah-coo'-hoo-dooh *adj., adv.* To the north.
Coo-nah-dis'-cah *adj., adv.* To the east.
Coo-nah-dis'-chooh *adj., adv.* To the west.
Coo-nah-ti-dooh *adj., adv.* To the south.
Coo-nah'-nooh *adj.* Doubtful.
Coo'-ne-sah'-ne-coo-ah *n.* Roof.
Coo-neh' *n.* House fly.
Coo-noo-ha-sah'-ah-coo *n.* Melon.
Coo-nooh-cah-ke-cus'-neh *n.* Pumpkin.
Coo-num-me'-tah *n.* Town.
Coo-ooh *n.* Worm.
Coo-ooh ha-e'-may *n.* Caterpillar.
Coo-sah'-yah *v.* Come eat.

Coo′-see-nah *adj., adv.* Enough (that's enough).
Coo′-tsa *v.* To have; to own.
Coo-um-me-coo′-sah *n.* Elbow.

Cooh

Cooh′-cooh *n.* Water.
Cooh′-cooh-ah-tsi-yo *n.* Sabine River.
Cooh-dee′ *v.* To move away.
Cooh′-weeh *n.* Early, spring grapes. *See* Kiss-weeh′.
Cooh′-whooh *n.* Alligator.
Cooh′-yah *n.* Rain.
Coot′-ne′-ah *n., v.* 1. Death (the formal term for human beings); 2. "He's gone."

Cu

Cum-bish′-nah-eeh *n.* Traditional Caddo dress; women's or girls' garment, with a waist and skirt.
Cun-ah-ho′-tsa-ah *n.* Air; also pronounced *ca′-ah-na-oat′-sa-ah.*
Cun-che′-bah *n.* Glass mirror.
Cun-che-bah cah-we′-cha-ah *n.* Window.
Cun-dut-ooh *n.* Mud.
Cun-o′-shun-nee *v.* To announce a dance.
Cus *n.* Hail.
Cus-see *n.* Beads. *See* Nah-kim-be.
Cus-see-nah-kim′-be *n.* Necklace.
Cup′-pah-a′ *n.* Horse fly.
Cut′ *n.* Knife.

Da

Da-cah′-ah *v.* To cry.
Da′-sah *v.* To lay.
Da-we′-dah-shah *v.* To jump.
Da′-nah *v., informal.* Do it.

Dah

Dah *n.* Deer.
Dah-bin *v.* To hit. *See* Cah-kee′-bin.
Dah-bus *n.* Beans, a variety similar to black beans. *See* Bah-hey′.

Dah′-cah′ *v.* To yell.
Dah-cush *v.* To cut. *See* Cah-kee′cush.
Dah-coo-cah-nit′-widish *n.* Soup.
Dah-cun′-co *n.* Purple.
Dah′-de-kee *v.* To go to sleep.
Dah-din′-neh *n.* Forest.
Dah′-e *v.* To give.
Dah-hung′-cah-hay *v.* You help. *See* Cah-kee-hung′-cah-hay.
Dah′-neh *n.* Muscle; sinew.
Dah′-nooh *v.* Pick it up.
Dah-noom′-bah-nah *v.* Tell him.
Dah-tooh *n.* Tripe.
Dah-wat′ *n.* Basket. *See* So′-yah.
Dah-we-us-ah′-bin *v.* To run.
Dah′-we-shah *v.* To get down.
Dah-yah′-cah *v.* Drink (command).
Dah-yea′-hoot *v.* Come in.
Dah-yeun′-nee *v.* To carry.
Dah-yo′-cah *v.* Get out!

De

De-ha-es-cum′-kee-sah *n.* Today.
De′-tooh-tse *n.* Pepper. *See* Cah-un′-cah-us.
Dee′-tum-ah ha′-tee-no *n.* Bay horse.
De′-tum-ah *n.* Horse or pony.
Dee-tooh *n.* Fart.
Dee′-tsi *n.* Dog.

Di

Dis′-cah *n.* Noon.
Dis-cah *n.* Noon-meal; lunch.
Dit-teh *adv.* Here; at this place.

Do

Do-kist′-tsi *n.* Sparrow hawk.
Do′-no-see *n.* Wool.
Do-noo-de′-tum-ah *n.* Stallion.
Do′-ooh *n.* Rabbit.

Doet'-cha-sun *adj.* Careful; done with close attention.
Dooh'-hooh' *adj.* Polk.
Doot'-ti-ti *n.* Colt.
Dough-cay'-bah *v.* To listen.
Dough'-cah-yah-nah-ah *v.* To talk.
Dough-oo-tay'-one *v.* To play.

Du

Dump'-mah' *v.* Bring it; get it.
Dump-mah'-nee *v.* To bring; get.
Dush'-cut *n.* Bread.
Dush'-cut nah-de'-cut *n.* Skillet bread; pan bread.
Dush'-cut-ti-ti *n.* Cookies; literally, "little bread."
Dush'-cut hah-beh'-tso *n.* Cake; literally, "sweet bread."
Dush-koon'-nah-ah *n.* Shadow.
Dush-tooh *n.* Ribbon headdress for women.
Dut' *n.* Mouse.

E

E-a'-ti-ti *n.* Older sister.
E-bit-dah-ah-ooh'-dah *interjection.* You are late.
E'-but *n.* Grandfather on the male side of the family.
E'-c'-cha *n.* Hand.
E-cah'-ti-ti *n.* Aunt by marriage.
E'-chew-eh *n.* Raisins.
E'-chun *n.* Frog.
Ee-cha' *n.* Ghost dance pole.
E'-ha-beh-tso *n.* Sweet potatoes.
E'-ha-cah-yooh *n.* White potatoes.
E'-ha-si-nai *n.* Wild potatoes of northwestern Louisiana and eastern Texas.
E'-kah *n.* Grandmother on the paternal side of the family.
E'-nah *n.* Mother.
E-nah-e'-may *n.* Older aunt on the maternal side of the family.
E'-nah-ha-ee-may *n.* Grandmother on the maternal side of the family.
E'-nah'-ti-ti *n.* Aunt on the maternal side of the family.
E'-nah-wah'-dut *n.* Earth; literally, "mother dirt."

E′-nay-ti-ti *n.* Younger uncle on the maternal side of the family.
E′-nee-cooh *n.* Mountain.
E-ney′-ti-ti *n.* Older brother.
E-wee′ *n.* Eagle.
E-yah-wut-see *n.* Antelope.
E-ish-e-que′-tah *n.* Apache band.
Eye-yah-hah-buh *n.* Hawk (large).

Ha

Ha-ace-cah-o′-tah-sah *n.* Sunrise.
Ha′-ah-hut *adj.* Good.
Ha-ba-la *adj.* Bad.
Ha-beh′-tsu wid′-dish *n.* Sugar.
Ha-cah-oh′ *n.* Bowl.
Ha-cah-seh′ *adj.* Worn out.
Ha-cah′-yo-sha′ *n.* Light-color horse.
Ha-cah′-yo cah-dus *n.* White comb. *See* Sue-nah.
Ha-choo-chun′-ta-me-sah *n.* Headache (I have a headache).
Ha-coo′-dooh *n., adj.* 1. Winter; 2. Cold.
Ha-coo′-nooh *adj.* Brown.
Ha-coo′-shoo *n., adj.* 1. Medicine; 2. Bitter.
Ha-cooh-sin *n.* Pinto horse.
Ha-cooh-sue *adj.* Big spots (horse).
Ha-dah′-chu *n.* Sharp pain. *See* Ha-e-yah-cah-oot-nooh.
Ha-de-cooh′ *adj., n.* 1. Black; 2. Black person.
Ha-deh′-coo-sha *n.* Dark colored (horse).
Ha-dun′-no-se *n.* Sweater.
Ha-dun′-ooh *n.* Syrup.
Ha-dush-cah-ah *adj.* Hard.
Ha-e-may′ *adj.* Big.
Ha-e-yah-cah-oot-nooh *n.* Dull pain. *See* Ha-dah′-chu.
Ha-ko′-ooh-sah *adj.* Awake.
Ha-no-coo′-ah-yah *n.* Soul.
Ha-ooh′-so *adj.* Gray.
Ha-sah′-cooh *adj.* Blue.
Ha-sah′-yooh cah-cum-me′-cha-ah *n.* Lard.
Ha-sah′-youh *adj.* Fat.
Ha-see′-ney *n.* Our people.

Ha-suck-a′-cah-yah-ah *adj.* Transparent; clear.
Ha-ti-nooh′ *n.* Amerindian people. *See* Ha-yah′-noh.
Ha-wah-in′ *n.* Ailment.
Ha-yah′-noh *n.* Human Amerindian people. *See* ha-ti-nooh′.

Hah

Hah′-ah-hut *adj.* Pretty good.
Hah-cah′-yoh *adj.* White.
Hah-coo′-shu hush-dun-ah *n.* Poison.
Hah-coo-tse-sah *n.* Illness.
Hah-sue-hoon′ *adj.* New.
Hah-te-dooh′ *adj.* Hot. *See* Nah′-teh-dooh.
Hah-te-nooh′ *adj.* Red.

Hay

Hay-in *n.* Daughter. *See* Hey′-en.
Hay′-nee-wah *n.* 1. Sheep; 2. Blanket.
Hay′-nee-wun′-ti *n.* Handkerchief.
Hay-she *adv.* Again.

He

He-coo′ *n.* Sea; gulf.
He-ooh′-soo *n.* Mist.
He-nah *n.* Snow.
He-nah-cah-kee-toosh′-ah *n.* Ice. *See* Cah-sue.
Hey′-en *n.* Daughter. *See* Hay-in.

Hi

Hi′-ya-shoo *n.* Monday.

Ho

Ho-kee-hun-noh′-sah *n.* Life; literally, "still breathing."
Ho′-tooh *n.* Wind.
Hoe′-tsa-ha *adj.* Different. *See* Hoosh′-nooh.
Hoosh′-nooh *adj.* Different. *See* Hoe′-tsa-ha.

Hu

Hah-ky′-coo *adj.* 1. Yellow; 2. Orange.
Hah-ky′-coo cah-bah-nine′-nah-ah *n.* Carrots; literally, "yellow roots."

Hah-ky′-coo cah-e-see-dun′-nah-ah *n.* Bananas.
Hun-nah-che *adj.* Difficult.
Hush-dun′-ah *adj.* Dangerous.

Ja
Ja-ca-do′-ah *n.* Rain crow.
Ja-ca-do′-ah ha-e-may *n.* Chaparral bird; roadrunner.

Ka
Ka′-ah-dus *n.* Comb.
Ka′-un-chee *n.* Granddaughter.
Kai′-a-cooh *n.* Drum.
Kay′-koh-tsi *n.* Bells.
Kayh′ *n.* Goose.

Ke
Kee′-cah *n.* Snake.
Kee′-dooh *n.* Toad.
Kee-nee-ti-ti *n.* Older brother.
Kee-o-nah wah′-wah ha-e-may′-chee *n.* Ancestors; the Old People.
Kee′-sheeh *n.* Leopard.
Kee-wut′ ha-e′-may *or* Kee-wut′-hi-u *n.* Heaven; "home above"; "big home."
Kee′-youh *n.* 1. Horn; 2. Spoon.
Kee-yun′-deh *n.* Candy.
Keeh-seeh *n.* Corn.

Ki
Kin-ee-see *n.* Canadian River.
Kin-nay′-ti-ti *n.* A female's brother.
Kish-sih′ cah-oh′-shun *n.* Corn dance.
Kish-wah′ *n.* Powdered corn.
Kiss-weeh′ *n.* Wild, small, fall grapes. *See* Cooh′-weeh.

Ko
Ko-ah′-cah *v.* He or she works up; creates.
Ko-dush′-ah *n.* Tree.
Ko-hout *n.* Grass.

Ku

Kuh′-dah-do′-uh-sin *n.* Stirrup dance; "one foot over the other."
Kun′-cooh *n.* Liver.
Kun′-tsi *n.* Head.
Kun′ *n.* Duck.

M

Me′-youh *n.* Cat.
Mun *n.* Heart.

Na

Na-say′-sah-cha *n.* This day.

Nah

Nah-cah-ca′-sah *n.* Plate.
Nah′-cah-cun-chah′-toh *n.* Suitcase.
Nah-cha-wi *n.* Angelina River.
Nah′-chooh *n.* Intestines.
Nah-coo′-dooh *n.* North (direction).
Nah′-cooh *n.* Bone. *See* Cah-ah-nah′-cha.
Nah′-cush *n.* Hog.
Nah-cush′-cha-yah *n.* Armadillo.
Nah-cush′-ti-ti *n.* Pig.
Nah-cut′-dah-hun *n.* Underwear.
Nah′-do-heh *n.* Ankle.
Nah-e-nun-chut′-dah-hun *n.* Socks.
Nah-he′-yah *n.* Pecans.
Nah-hey′-be *n.* Apron.
Nah-kee *v.* To look at oneself.
Nah-kee-bim′-beh *n.* Tie.
Nah-kee-cah′-son *n.* Dress.
Nah-kee-cah′-son-cah-coo-tas-ah *n.* Blouse.
Nah-kee-cah-son′-cah-we′-cha-ah *n.* Dress material.
Nah-kee-cah′-son-shoo-we *n.* Shirt.
Nah-kee-cah′-tooh *n.* Heater.
Nah-kee-cha-nee-coh′-tu-weh *n.* Water glasses.
Nah-kee-cah′-win-nah *n.* Weight.
Nah-kee-toon-cha′-son *n.* Pants.

Nah-kee-hun′-nah cah-bin′-nah *n.* Stove for cooking food.
Nah-kee′-hush-no′ eh-ah-cha *n.* Table.
Nah-kee-kim′-be *n.* Drum dance.
Nah-kee′-nah-sin-cha *n.* Bracelet.
Nah-kee′-sah *n.* Bed.
Nah-kee′-soot *n.* Sewing machine.
Nah-kee′-shu *n.* Pencil.
Nah-kee′-toh-cah′-yatch-ah *n.* Wooden chair.
Nah-kee-tsu′-wit *n.* Earring.
Nah-kee-wah-ti′-cha *n.* Fork.
Nah-kee-win′-cha *n.* Skirt.
Nah-kee′-yah *n.* Food.
Nah-keen′-cah-nah *n.* Match.
Nah-kim-be *n.* Beads. *See* Cus-see.
Nah-kim-be′-tse *n.* Pillow.
Nah-kin-oon′-uh-nah *n.* Fan.
Nah-kin-che′-bin *n.* 1. Belt; 2. Buckle.
Nah-nee′-sah′-nah *n.* Ghost dance (Arapaho) introduced into Indian Territory in 1890.
Nah-sah-cah-koe′-we *n.* Fall; "when the leaves begin to fall."
Nah-say′-ta-nah-hon′-dah *n.* Next week.
Nah′-shee *n.* Big acorns.
Nah-seeh′ *n.* Kidney.
Nah′-shooh *n.* Foot.
Nah′-teh-dooh *n.* Hot. *See* Hah-te-dooh′.
Nah-ti-dooh *n.* South. *See* Coo-nah-ti-dooh.
Nah′-tso-nee *n.* Appaloosa horse.
Nah′-we *adv.* Down.
Nah-wi′-dish-da-ah *adj.* "Show-off."
Nah′-yah-cooh′ *v.* To dream. *See* Yah′-cooh′.
Nah-yah-we-coo′-tah *n.* Box.

Nate

Nate′-dah-yun-ha *n.* Policeman.
Nate′-dah-yun-nush′-ah-ha *n.* Nurse.
Nate′-tsi nah-cah-wish-ah *n.* Husband; "companion around the fire."
Nate′-tso-tah-nee′-ah *n.* Fighting companion (jokingly).

Nay

Nay′wah-chee *n.* Mouth.

Nee

Nee′-coo-hey *n.* Back.
Nee′-cooh *n.* Fire.
Nee-dah′-heh *n.* Stream.
Nee-hee *n.* White owl. *See* Cah-e-tsi.
Nee-ot′-tsi *n.* Road.
Nee-tooh *n.* Feather.
Nee-we′-sooh *n.* Arm.
Neesh *n.* Moon.
Nees′-choo *n.* Yesterday.

Nit

Nit-ah-cah-oh′ *adj.* Boiled.
Nit-tso-sah-dos-cha-ah *n.* Chairman; "one who sits in the chair."

No

Nooh′ *n.* Turkey.
Nooh′-cah-o′-shun-nah *n.* Turkey dance.
Noos′-bick-ooh *n.* Eggs.
Note′-chey *n.* Calf; fleshy area of the leg below the knee.
Note′-tsi *n.* Bear.

Nu

Nup′-bah *n.* Night.
Nush′-tu *n.* Newspaper.
Nut′-see-heh *n.* Neck.
Nut′-teh-tsi *n.* Girl; "little woman."

O

Oh-ah-hee *n.* Pawnee.
One′-teh *adj.* All of it.
Ooh-bah *n.* 1. Cottonwood (tree); 2. Slabs.
Ooth hah-cah′-yo *n.* Badger.
Oot′ *n.* Raccoon.

Sah

Sah'-ah *n.* Box elder tree.
Sah'-ah-nah-nooh *v.* To be hungry (I am hungry).
Sah'-cah-heh *n.* Wall.
Sah-cooh *n.* Sun.
Sah-chu-ooh'-nooh *n.* Daughter-in-law.
Sah'-cup-peh *n.* Coffee pot.
Sah-dah'-cha-ah *n.* Boots.
Sah'-dah-neh *n.* Bucket.
Sah'-ha *n.* Walnut tree.
Sah'-hah-cah-cun-ney'-ah *n.* Walnuts.
Sah'-sin de'-tum-ah *n.* Mare.
Sah-yah-ti *n.* Old lady.
Sah-yo-dah-ney'-ah *n.* Twins. *See* Chah'-dooh.

Say

Say'-wah-che *n.* Centipede.

S

Se-na-tun'-kah *interjection, informal.* That's the way it goes.
Se-seh' *n.* Flea.
See-ah-nah'-bo *n.* Cheyenne.
See-kung'-cah-hey *n.* Palm.
See'-neeh *n.* Blackjack oak tree.
Sha-wa'-no *n.* Shawnee.
She-ah'-tsi *n.* Boy.
She-wah' *n.* Squirrel.
Shoo'-we *n.* Man.
Sic'-ooh *n.* Rock.
Sho'nah *n.* Moss.
Sho'nah Es-pah-yoon' *n.* Spanish moss.
Sim'-bit-tooh *n.* Finger.
Sit-to-tie'-yah-kin-eoh-nah *n.* Length of time.
So'-yah *n.* Basket. *See* Dah-wat'.
Sue-heh *n.* Plains.
Sue-nah or Sue'-nah *n.* 1. Comb; 2. Silver money; 3. Money.
Sun'-cha-neh *n.* Dish pan.
Swee *n.* Hawk.

Tah

Tah′-nah-ha *n.* Buffalo.
Tah′-ooh *n.* Beaver.
Ta′-sha *n.* 1. Wolf; 2. Friend.

Tay

Tay-ti-ti *n.* Younger sister.

Tee

Tee-dut *n.* Ant.

Ts

Tsa-do′-oot *n.* Prairie dog.
Tsa′-e-yah-ti *adj.* "In the morning."
Tsa′-ha-e-yah *n.* Tomorrow.
Tsa-kee′-yooh *n.* Devil.
Tsa-nee-a′-dah-cha *n.* Mountain lion.
Tsa-tah′-win *n.* Possum.
Tsa-ip bah′-kin *n.* Son-in-law.
Tsah′-cub-be *n.* February.
Tsah-toeh *n.* Rat.
Tse-nee *n.* Nothing.
Tso-bah′-cush *n.* Sioux; literally, "cutthroat."
Tsoo′-tsoo′ *n.* Milk.
Tsoo-tsoo dush′-cut *n.* Cheese; literally, "milk bread."
Tsoo-tsoo ha-sah′-yooh *n.* Butter.
Tsu′-cus *n.* Stars.
Tswe′-dah-neh *n.* Cup.

Tu

Tu′-we-ti-ti *n.* Younger brother.
Tum′-mah *n.* Camp cryer; town cryer.
Tun-ut *n.* Grasshopper.
Tus′-seeh′ *n.* Spider.

Us

Us′ *n.* Persimmon.

Wah

Wah-ah *n.* Bee.

Wah-ah ha'-ti-nooh *n.* Wasp.

Wah-cus *n.* 1. Cow; 2. Beef. *See* Cah-oo'-tooh.

Wah'-dooh' *n.* Bobcat; wild cat.

Wah-dut *n.* Dirt.

Wah'-hee *n.* Shoes.

Wah'-sha-nee'-kee *n.* Second segment of the drum dance. *See* Nah-kee-kim'-be.

Wah-shush *n.* Osage drum dance.

We

We-tum'-mah-dah-ah *adj.* Bashful (He is bashful).

Wee-hit' *n.* Skunk.

Wee-ut *n.* Elk.

Weh'-dish *n.* 1. Salt; 2. (informal) Cute.

Weh'-ish *n.* Sand.

Wi

Wi'-dish-nah-kee-cun'-nah-nah *n.* Soup.

Wis'-keeh *n.* Whiskey.

Wis'-nah'-win *n.* Rainbow.

Yah

Yah'-ah *n.* Summer.

Yah'-cooh *n.* Wood.

Yah-cooh' *v., n.* 1. To dream (*see* Nah-yah-cooh'); 2. "Sleepyhead."

Yah-cooh'-ti-ti *n.* "Little sleepyhead."

NOTES

CHAPTER ONE

1. The thoughts of Francis Williams, Melford Williams, and Irving Whitebead are reflected in this discussion of the origins and early migrations of the Hasinai. These ideas may be compared with materials presented in published form in George A. Dorsey's *Traditions of the Caddo* (Washington, D.C.: Carnegie Institution of Washington, 1905) and John R. Swanton's *Source Material on the History and Ethnology of the Caddo Indians* (Smithsonian Institution, Bureau of American Ethnology, Bulletin 132 [Washington, D.C.: U.S. Government Printing Office, 1942]).

CHAPTER TWO

1. *Cultural Resources Evaluation of the North Gulf of Mexico Continental Shelf* (2 vols., Washington, D.C.: National Park Service, U.S. Department of the Interior, 1977), I, pp. 148–169.

2. The thoughts of George Beaver are reflected in this discussion of meat preservation. It can be compared with information in Fannie Hudson Interview and Sadie Bedoka Interview, Indian Archives, Oklahoma Historical Society, Oklahoma City, Oklahoma.

CHAPTER THREE

1. The thoughts of George Beaver are reflected in this discussion of agriculture.

2. See Herbert E. Bolton, "The Native Tribes about the East Texas Missions," *Quarterly of the Texas State Historical Association,* 11 (1908), pp. 249–276; H. F. Gregory, *Excavations: Presidio de Nuestra Señora del Pilar de los Adaes* (Baton Rouge: Louisiana Department of Culture, Tourism, and Recreation, 1980); William J. Griffith, *The Hasinai Indians of East Texas as Seen by Europeans, 1687–1772,* Middle American Research Institute, Philiological and Documentary Series, 2 (New Orleans: Tulane University, 1954); H. Perry Newell and Alex D. Krieger, "The George C. Davis Site, Cherokee County, Texas," *Memoirs*

of the Society for American Archaeology (1949), pp. 241–249; Dee Ann Story, ed., *Archeological Investigations at the George C. Davis Site, Cherokee County, Texas: Summers of 1979–1980* (Austin: Texas Archeological Research Laboratory, Occasional Papers No. 1, 1981); Swanton, *Source Material.*

CHAPTER FOUR

1. Caddo communities varied in size from as few as five and six structures to larger ones with hundreds of houses, arbors, and storage structures. The Domingo Teran map of 1691–1692 pictures a Caddo village of twenty-five clusters of buildings. The original map is in the Archivo General de Indias, Seville, Spain; a copy is printed in Frank F. Schambach and Frank Rackerby, eds., "Contributions to the Archeology of the Great Bend Region of the Red River Valley, Southwest Arkansas," *Arkansas Archeological Survey Research Series,* 22 (1982), pp. 6–7. This publication also reproduces two photographs of Caddo farmsteads taken in 1868 and 1872 (p. 8).

2. See Clarence H. Webb, "Housing Types Among the Caddo Indians," *Texas Archeological and Paleontological Society,* pp. 49–75; Benny J. Wallace, "Prehistoric House Patterns of Oklahoma," *Oklahoma Anthropological Society Publications,* pp. 27–68.

3. See Dee Ann Story, ed., *Archeological Investigations at the George C. Davis Site, Cherokee County, Texas, Summers of 1979 and 1980* (Austin: Texas Archeological Research Laboratory, Occasional Papers No. 1, 1981).

4. See J. Daniel Rogers, Michael C. Moore, and Rusty Greaves, *Spiro Archaeology: The Plaza* (Norman: Oklahoma Archaeology Survey, 1982).

CHAPTER FIVE

1. See Fray Juan Agustín de Morfi, *Excerpts from the Memorias for the History of the Province of Texas* (n.p., 1932); Pierre Margry, *Découvertes et établissements des Français dans l'ouest et dans le sud de l'Amérique* (Paris: n.p., 1875–1886); Fray Francisco Casañas de Jesús María, "Descriptions of the Tejas or Asinai Indians, 1691–1722," translated by Mattie Austin Hatcher, *Southwestern Historical Quarterly,* 30, pp. 206–218, 283–304; Fray Isidro Felís de Espinosa, "Descriptions of the Tejas or Asinai Indians, 1691–1722," translated by Mattie Austin Hatcher, *Southwestern Historical Quarterly,* 31, pp. 150–180; Griffith, *The Hasinai Indians of East Texas as Seen by Europeans, 1687–1772;* Swanton, *Source Material.*

CHAPTER SIX

1. See Leslie Spier, "Wichita and Caddo Relationship Terms," *American Anthropologist,* 26 (April–June, 1924), pp. 258–263; Elsie Clews Parsons, *Notes on the Caddo, Memoirs of the American Anthropological Association,* 57 (1941), pp.

11–23, 28–31; Swanton, *Source Material,* pp. 159–161; Mrs. Frank Cussins [*sic*] [Cussen] Interview, Indian-Pioneer Papers, Indian Archives, Oklahoma Historical Society, Oklahoma City, Oklahoma.

CHAPTER SEVEN

1. William W. Newcomb, *The Indians of Texas from Prehistoric to Modern Times* (Austin: University of Texas Press, 1969), p. 303.

2. There is comparative literature from the seventeenth and eighteenth centuries in manuscript form collected in archives at the University of Texas at Austin and the University of California at Berkeley. These include writings of Fray Francisco Casañas de Jesús María, Fray Francisco de Celíz, Fray Isidro Felix de Espinosa, Fray Francisco Hidalgo, Fray Damian Massanet, Fray Antonio de San Buenaventura Olivares, Louis Juchereau de St. Denis, Fray Gaspar José de Solis. Additional colonial materials are housed at the Stephen F. Austin State University at Nacogdoches, Texas, and Northwest Louisiana State University at Nachitoches, Louisiana. Two helpful published sources on governance are Griffith's *The Hasinai,* and Don G. Wycoff and Timothy G. Baugh, "Early Historic Hasinai Elites: A Model for the Material of Governing Elites," *Mid-Continental Journal of Archaeology,* 5 (1980), pp. 225–288.

3. See Clarence H. Webb and Hiram F. Gregory, *The Caddo of Louisiana,* Anthropological Study No. 2 (Baton Rouge: Department of Culture, Recreation, and Tourism, Louisiana Archaeological Survey and Antiquities Commission, 1978) for materials relating to the peace and moderation that resulted from mutual cultural accommodations.

CHAPTER EIGHT

1. See also Mattie Austin Hatcher, "Descriptions of the Tejas or Asinai Indians, 1691–1722," *Southwestern Historical Quarterly,* 30 (January 1927), pp. 206–218; ibid. (April 1927), pp. 283–304; ibid., 31 (July 1927), pp. 50–62; ibid. (October 1927), pp. 150–180; Bolton, "The Native Tribes"; Lawrence Kinnaird, "Spanish Treaties with Indian Tribes," *Western Historical Quarterly,* 10 (January 1979), pp. 39–48; William B. Glover, "A History of the Caddo Indians," *Louisiana Historical Quarterly,* 18 (1935), pp. 872–945; Caddo Agency Files, 1824–1833 and 1824–1843, microfilm, Library, Oklahoma Historical Society, Oklahoma City, Oklahoma; Mrs. Lee C. Harby, "The Tejas: Their Habits, Government, and Superstitions," *Annual Report of the American Historical Association* (Washington, D.C.: U.S. Government Printing Office, 1894), pp. 63–82; Kenneth F. Neighbours, "Robert S. Neighbors and the Founding of Texas Indian Reservations," *West Texas Historical Association Year Book,* 31 (October 1955), pp. 65–74; Republic of Texas Indian Affairs Files, Texas State Library, Austin, Texas; Berlin B. Chapman, "Establishment of the Wichita Reservation," *Chronicles of Oklahoma,* 11 (December 1933), pp. 1044–1055.

2. See Henri Joutel, *The Last Voyage Performed by de la Salle* (London: A. Bell, 1714), and Ralph A. Smith, trans. and ed., "Account of the Journey of Ber-

nard de la Harpe: Discovery Made by Him of Several Nations Situated in the West," *Southwestern Historical Quarterly,* 62 (July 1968), pp. 250–251; Webb and Gregory, *The Caddo.*

3. In addition to oral testimony in the Indian-Pioneer Papers, Indian Archives, Oklahoma Historical Society, Oklahoma City, Oklahoma, and Duke Oral History Collection, Western History Collections, University of Oklahoma, Norman, Oklahoma, see Elizabeth A. H. John, *Storms Brewed in Other Men's Worlds: The Confrontations of Indians, Spanish, and French in the Southwest, 1540–1795* (College Station: Texas A&M University Press, 1975), pp. 157–195, 203–224, 344–346; Griffith, *The Hasinai,* pp. 135–152.

4. Mary Idanish [*sic*] (Inkanish) Interview, C. Ross Hume Collection, Western History Collections, University of Oklahoma, Norman, Oklahoma.

5. Jehiel Brooks to E. Herring, Natchitoches, Louisiana, September 15, 1830; Jehiel Brooks to John Eaton, Natchitoches, Louisiana, September 17, 1830; Jehiel Brooks to E. Herring, Caddo Prairie, Louisiana, February 13, 1832; Jehiel Brooks to E. Herring, Caddo Prairie, Louisiana, April 4, 1833; Jehiel Brooks to E. Herring, Caddo Prairie, Louisiana, April 9, 1833; Jehiel Brooks to E. Herring, Annual Report, November 23, 1833; Jehiel Brooks to E. Herring, Caddo Prairie, Louisiana, July 10, 1834, Letters Received from the Caddo Agency, National Archives, Washington, D.C.

6. Treaty of Bird's Fort, September 29, 1843, *Texas Indian Papers,* James M. Day, ed. (3 vols., Austin: Texas State Library, 1969), I, pp. 241–245.

7. Minutes of the Indian Council at Tehuacana Creek, March 28, 1843, *Texas Indian Papers,* I, p. 160.

8. See "Report of R. B. Marcy and R. S. Neighbors to P. H. Bell," *Texas Indian Papers,* III, p. 188, and Kenneth F. Neighbors, "José María: Anardarko Chief," *Chronicles of Oklahoma,* 46 (Fall 1966), pp. 254–274.

9. Neighbors Invoice, July 30, 1859; Matthew Leeper to Elias Rector, Annual Report, September 26, 1860; Matthew Leeper to Capt. Gilbert, Wichita Agency, Indian Territory, December 28, 1860, Letters Received by the Commissioner of Indian Affairs from the Wichita Agency, National Archives, Washington, D.C.; C. Ross Hume, "Historical Sites Around Anadarko," *Chronicles of Oklahoma,* 16 (1938), p. 412; Elias Rector to A. B. Greenwood, *Reports of the Commissioner of Indian Affairs, 1859* (Washington: U.S. Government Printing Office, 1936), p. 332.

10. Kenneth F. Neighbours, "Indian Exodus Out of Texas," *West Texas Historical Association Year Book,* 36 (1960), pp. 84–85.

11. Notes of Council at White Waters, October 14, 1864; Elias Sills to D. N. Cooley, Wichita Agency, Indian Territory, November 15, 1865, Letters Received from Wichita Agency.

12. See Henry Shanklin to Wortham, Annual Report, November 3, 1867, Letters Received from the Wichita Agency; Cheyenne *Transporter,* June 25, 1881; ibid., March 27, 1883; ibid., February 20, 1886; *Cherokee Advocate* (Tahlequah), April 7, 1882; El Reno *News,* June 19, 1896; ibid., July 2, 1897; ibid., June 24, 1898; ibid., July 7, 1899; R. L. Boake Interview, Indian-Pioneer Papers, Indian Archives, Oklahoma Historical Society, Oklahoma City, Oklahoma; Tomas C. Battey, *The Life and Adventures of a Quaker Among the Indians* (Norman: University of Oklahoma Press, 1968); Lawrie Tatum, *Our Red Brothers and the Peace Policy*

of President Ulysses S. Grant (Lincoln: University of Nebraska Press, 1970).

13. Eli Wilson, at the request of George Washington (Caddo), to Nelson A. Miles, Wichita Agency, Indian Territory, August 23, 1874, Letters Received from the Wichita Agency; "Speech by Tyner (Caddo) at the Okmulgee Council, June, 1875; Williams to Commissioner, Kiowa Agency, Indian Territory, April 4, 1877, Kiowa Agency Letterbook 15, Indian Archives, Oklahoma Historical Society, Oklahoma City, Oklahoma; Billie Wilson Deposition, Indian-Pioneer Papers.

14. Communication of White Bead [*sic*] to the President of the United States, February 3, 1888, Hume Collection. The communication was dictated by Whitebread, the Hasinai *cah-de*.

15. Edmond *Sun-Democrat*, May 14, 1891; ibid., May 14, 1897; Oklahoma *Times-Journal*, February 5, 1892; Lexington *Leader*, March 12, 1892; Kingfisher *Free Press*, July 7, 1892; El Reno *News*, March 12, 1897; Blackwell *Times-Record*, March 24, 1898; Woodward *News*, March 25, 1899; Alva *Review*, March 2, 1901; ibid., August 15, 1901; ibid., August 13, 1903; Chickasha *Daily Express*, June 26, 1901; *Cherokee Advocate* (Tahlequah), July 13, 1901; Stillwater *Advance*, October 23, 1902; Carleton Ross Hume Interview, Indian-Pioneer Papers.

16. *Corporate Charter of the Caddo Indian Tribe of Oklahoma, Ratified November 15, 1938* (Washington: U.S. Government Printing Office, 1939); *Constitution and By-laws of the Caddo Indian Tribe of Oklahoma, Ratified January 17, 1938* (Washington: U.S. Government Printing Office, 1938); *Daily Oklahoman* (Oklahoma City), January 19, 1938.

17. *Constitution and By-Laws of the Caddo Indian Tribe of Oklahoma* (as ratified June 26, 1976), in *Constitution and By-Laws*, compiled by Andrew Skeeter (Anadarko: Anadarko Area Office of the Bureau of Indian Affairs, c. 1985).

CHAPTER NINE

1. Swanton, *Source Material*, p. 224.

2. Francis Williams Interview, translated by Melford Williams, Hasinai Cultural Center, Norman, Oklahoma.

3. Compare these concepts with those recorded in Swanton's *Source Material*, pp. 203–209, 226–233; Elsie Clews Parsons, "Notes on the Caddo," *Memoirs of the American Anthropological Association*, No. 57 (Menasha: American Anthropological Association, 1941), pp. 32–39.

CHAPTER TEN

1. *The Caddoan, Iroquoian, and Siouan Languages* (The Hague: Mouton, 1976); "Caddoan" in *The Languages of Native America: Historical and Comparative Assessment*, Lyle Campbell and Marianne Mithun, eds. (Austin: University of Texas Press, 1979).

2. Swanton, *Source Material*, p. 176.

3. Chaffe, *Caddoan, Iroquoian, and Siouan Languages*, pp. 64–82; idem, "Caddoan," pp. 228–29.

CHAPTER ELEVEN

1. *Daily Oklahoman* (Oklahoma City), October 22, 1978.
2. *Constitution and By-Laws*, Whitebead Hasinai Cultural Center, Norman, Oklahoma.

CHAPTER TWELVE

1. Recordings of the turkey dance songs are available in the Duke Oral History Collection in the Western History Collections at the University of Oklahoma in Norman, Oklahoma, and in the tapes recorded by the Whitebead Hasinai Cultural Center, "Songs of the Caddo" (2 vols., Phoenix: Canyon Records, 1976), with Lowell "Wimpey" Edmonds, Leon Carter, Houston Edmonds, Hubert Halfmoon, Irving Whitebead, Reuben Whitebead, and Melford Williams as the singers.
2. See Margery P. Gray and William S. Laughlin, "Blood Groups of Caddoan Indians of Oklahoma," *American Journal of Human Genetics*, 12 (1960), pp. 86–94.
3. See Paul C. Mangelsdorf, Richard S. MacNeish, and Walton C. Galinot, "Domestication of Corn," *Science*, 143 (February 7, 1964), pp. 538–545; P. C. Mangelsdorf and R. G. Reeves, "The Origin of Indian Corn and Its Relatives," *Texas Agricultural Experiment Station Bulletin*, no. 574 (1939); H. C. Dethloff and Irving M. May, Jr., *Southwestern Agriculture* (College Station: Texas A&M University Press, 1982).
4. Jesse D. Jennings and Edward Norbeck, eds., *Prehistoric Man in the New World* (Chicago: University of Chicago Press, 1971), p. 274.
5. This closing uses the Hasinai prayer language. It is used here as a closing prayer, for this is the form of this work.

SUGGESTIONS FOR FURTHER READING

The principal basis of this study of the Hasinai is the collective memory of the Hasinai people. This has been expressed in ceremonial song and dance, conversation, interviews, as well as Hasinai manuscript records and agencies of the United States government. The dance ground is the center of Hasinai tribal thought. The songs, dances, prayers, and personal conversations over the years formed the core of thought that defines this book. The home life of the several Caddo families mentioned in the notes rounded out the information and subject matter.

In addition, oral historical records exist for Hasinai studies. These are included in the Indian-Pioneer Papers housed in the Oklahoma Historical Society as a part of the Indian Archives in Oklahoma City, especially the Mrs. Frank Cussen Interview, the Fannie Hudson Crowell Interview, the Sadie Bedoka Interview, the Billie Wilson Deposition, and the Carleton Ross Hume Interview. More recent materials are contained in the Doris Duke Oral Indian History Collection in the Western History Collections, University of Oklahoma, Norman, Oklahoma, especially the Saddie Weller Interview, the Melford Williams Speech, the Lillie Hoag Whitehorn Interview, and the Andrew Dunlap Interview. Many of the songs of the Hasinai dances are included in the Duke Collection and are available at the Hasinai Cultural Center. Of the interviews on tape held by a member of the Hasinai Cultural Center, the most helpful is that of Francis Williams, which was translated by Melford Williams.

Unpublished colonial European materials describing Hasinai practices and culture are housed in collections throughout the southwest. The Bexar Archives and the Nacogdoches Archives at the University of Texas at Austin contain important materials related to Spanish-Hasinai relationships in the colonial era. The Texas Indian Papers and the Thomas J. Rusk Papers include manuscripts important for understanding Texas-Hasinai relationships. These are housed at the Texas State Archives in Austin. The C. Ross Hume Collection in the Western History Collections at the University of Oklahoma at Norman contains information concerning United States–Hasinai relationships, including early twentieth-century claims of the Caddo against the United States government. Spanish and French colonial documents are being collected and translated at Northwest Louisiana State University in Nachitoches. U.S. policy toward the Hasinai confederacy is outlined in the records of the Office of Indian Affairs and the records of the Quartermaster General, housed in the National Archives in Washington. The Letters Received from the Caddo Agency, 1824–1840, and Letters Received from the Wichita Agency, 1857–1875, as well as the Consolidated Correspondence, Fort Washita, 1834–1876, are particularly helpful to this end. The Collected Papers of the Wichita and Affiliated Tribes and the Caddo Tribe of Oklahoma in the Indian Archives of the Oklahoma Historical Society are helpful in understanding the difficult problems of the nineteenth century.

Published materials bring added light to U.S. and Texas relationships with the Hasinai. These include *Testimony Concerning the Caddo Indian Treaty of 1835,* House Document No. 25, 27th Congress, 2nd Session (1841), which describes the role of the United States Indian agent and intended payments to the Caddo. Additional information concerning the treaty of 1835 is included in the *Report of the Committee on Indian Affairs Concerning Fraud Committed by Commissioner Negotiating Caddo Indian Treaty of July 1, 1835,* Senate Report 199, Document 252, 27th Congress, 2nd Session (1842). The issues of *Report of the Commissioner of Indian Affairs, 1845–1883* provide a sense of the unrelenting pressure of the U.S. government upon the Caddo people in the southwest. The *Memorial of the Wichita, Caddo, and Affiliated Tribes of Indians, submitted February 25, 1892,* Senate Executive Document No. 46, 52nd Congress, 1st Session (1892) provides a brief history of U.S. dealings with the Wichita, Caddo, and other tribes that came out of Texas and Louisiana. A report concerning the treaty of 1846 is contained in *Texas Indians—Reports of Messes. Butler and Lewis,* House Executive Document No. 76, 29th Congress, 2nd Session (1847).

There are many ethnological, archeological, and linguistic materials on the Hasinai. A number of recent archeological investigations have produced interesting commentary on the material culture of the region of the Hasinai. One of the important early works is H. P. Newell and A. D. Krieger, *The George C. Davis Site, Cherokee County, Texas,* Society for American Archaeology, Memoirs, 5 (1949), pp. 1–271, which describes the remains of the important mound complex in the Neches River valley. In the summer of 1982, Vynola and I visited the site. She was most interested in the blackberry vines that abound there, as well as the variety of grasses. More recent excavations of the site are described in Dee Ann Story, ed., *Archeological Investigations at the George C. Davis Site, Cherokee County, Texas, Summers of 1979 and 1980,* Texas Archeological Research Laboratory Occasional Papers No. 1 (Austin: University of Texas at Austin, 1981). Another recent site investigation in the Angelina drainage area was recorded in Dee Ann Story, ed., *The Deshazo Site, Nacogdoches County, Texas* (Austin: Texas Antiquities Committee, 1982). Other Caddoan sites have been described in detail. Among the most informative are James A. Brown and Robert E. Bell, *The First Annual Report of Caddoan Archaeology, Spiro Focus Research* (Norman: University of Oklahoma Research Institute, 1964), which describes the architecture of the mounds at the Spiro site; J. Daniel Rogers, Michael C. Moore, and Rusty Greaves, *Spiro Archaeology: The Plaza* (Norman: Oklahoma Archaeological Survey, 1982); J. Daniel Rogers, *Spiro Archaeology: 1980 Research* (Norman: Oklahoma Archaeology Survey, 1982); J. Daniel Rogers, *Spiro Archaeology: 1979 Excavations* (Norman: Oklahoma Archaeological Survey, 1980); and Guy Muto, *The Habiukut of Eastern Oklahoma: Parris Mound* (Oklahoma City: Oklahoma Historical Society, 1978).

Four summary articles are helpful for putting archeological and ethnographic information into context. The first two are Clarence H. Webb and Hiram F. Gregory, *The Caddo Indians of Louisiana,* Anthropological Study No. 2 (Baton Rouge: Department of Culture,

Recreation, and Tourism, Louisiana Archaeological Survey and Antiquities Commission, 1978), and E. Davis Mott, "The Caddoan Area: An Introduction . . . ," *Texas Archaeology Society Bulletin,* 31, pp. 3–10. Two more extensive articles are Dee Ann Shuhm and Alex D. Krieger, "East Texas," *Bulletin of the Texas Archeological Society,* 25 (1954), pp. 144–227, and W. W. Newcomb, Jr., "Indian Tribes of Texas," *Bulletin of the Texas Archeological Society,* 29 (1960), pp. 25–62.

Several published works provide background in classic architectural styles in the Caddoan area. Archeological evidence is discussed in Hiram F. Gregory, "Los Adaes: The Archaeology of an Ethnic Enclave," *Geoscience and Man,* 23 (April 29, 1983), pp. 53–57, which describes the investigation of the summer of 1982. Older studies include C. H. Webb, "House Types among the Caddo Indians," *Texas Archeological and Paleontological Society,* Bulletin 12 (1940), pp. 49–75; B. J. Wallace, "Prehistoric House Patterns of Oklahoma," *Bulletin of the Oklahoma Anthropological Society,* 10 (1962), pp. 27–68; E. N. Wilmsen, "A Suggested Development Sequence for House Forms in the Caddoan Area," *Bulletin of the Texas Archaeological Society,* 30 (1959), pp. 35–49. Comparisons of classic and modern architectural styles may be found in F. H. Douglas, *The Grass House of the Wichita and Caddo,* Denver Art Museum, Indian Leaflets, Series I, No. 42 (1932), pp. 1–4; Frank F. Schambach and Frank Rackerby, eds., *Contributions to the Archeology of the Great Bend Region of the Red River Valley, Southwest Arkansas,* Arkansas Archeological Survey Research Series 22 (1982); and H. L. and Mary Ellen Meredith, eds., *Of the Earth: Oklahoma Architectural History* (Oklahoma City: Oklahoma Historical Society, 1980).

The Hasinai language is of critical importance to the understanding of Hasinai culture and civilization. The most helpful studies of Hasinai have been conducted by Jess Ahdunko, Sadie Bedoka, Ellen Edge Williams, Phil and Vynola Beaver Newkumet. The Glossary in this volume is the lifelong work of the Newkumets. Published studies include the work of Wallace L. Chafe in *The Languages of Native America: Historical and Comparative Assessment,* edited by Lyle Campbell and Marianne Mithun (Austin: University of Texas Press, 1979), pp. 213–235; *Caddoan Texts,* edited by Douglas R. Parks (Chicago: University of Chicago Press, 1977), pp. 27–43; *The Caddoan, Iroquoian, and Siouan Languages* (The Hague: Mouton, 1976), and "The Ordering of Phonological Rules," *International Journal of American Linguistics,* 34 (1968), pp. 115–137. Comparison with Hasinai may be made with the following: J. Sibley, "Vocabulary of the Caddoquis or Caddo Language," *American Naturalist* (1879), pp. 787–790, and Rudolph C. Troike, "The Caddo Word for 'Water,'" *International Journal of American Linguistics,* 30 (1964), pp. 96–98. Attempts have been made to classify Hasinai with other Caddoan languages in Allan R. Taylor, "The Classification of the Caddoan Languages," *American Philosophical Society, Proceedings,* 107 (1963), pp. 51–59, and Alexander Lesser and Gene Weltfish, *Composition of the Caddoan Linguistic Stock* (Washington: Smithsonian Institution, 1932).

Ethnographic and ethnohistorical studies are available in published form, providing a basis for comparison with contemporary Hasinai history and custom. Probably the most widely cited work is that of John R. Swanton, *Source Material on the History and Ethnology of the Caddo Indians,* Smithsonian Institution, Bureau of American Ethnology Bulletin 132 (Washington: U.S. Government Printing Office, 1942). This is a broadly based study, including translations of colonial materials on the Hasinai. Swanton also wrote "Caddo Social Organization and Its Possible Historical Significance," *Journal of the Washington Academy of Sciences,* 21 (1931), pp. 203–206. This should be compared to Don G. Wyckoff and Timothy G. Baugh, "Early Historic Hasinai Elites: A Model for the Material Culture of Governing Elites," *Midcontinental Journal of Archaeology,* 5 (1980), pp. 225–288. Elsie Clews Parsons' *Notes on the Caddo,* Memoirs of the American Anthropological Association No. 57 (1941) contains information gathered in 1921 and 1922. She noted the growing number of intertribal marriages at that time, with the exclusion of traditional enemies – Wichita, Osage, and Apache. This study and the Swanton work also contain folktales. These should be read in context with those collected in George A. Dorsey, *Traditions of the Caddo* (Washington: Carnegie Institution, 1905) and those in *Caddoan Texts,* cited earlier. Other collections of Hasinai texts include C. E. Castaneda, "Myths and Customs of the Tejas Indians," *Publication of the Texas Folk-lore Society,* 9 (1931), pp. 167–174; Mary Austin Hatcher, "Myths of the Tejas

Indians," *Publication of the Texas Folk-lore Society,* 4 (1927), pp. 107–118; and A. de Zavala, "Religious Beliefs of the Tejas or Hasanias Indians," *Publication of the Texas Folk-lore Society,* 1 (1916), pp. 39–43. Additional ethnological information was published in Mrs. L. C. Harby, "The Tejas: Their Habits, Government, and Superstitions," *Annual Report of the American Historical Association* (1894), pp. 63–82; George A. Dorsey, "Caddo Customs of Childhood," *Journal of American Folklore,* 18 (1905), pp. 226–228; Leslie Spier, "Wichita and Caddo Relationship Terms," *American Anthropologist,* New Series, 26 (1924), pp. 258–263, and E. Heflin, "The Oashuns or Dances of the Caddo," *Oklahoma Anthropological Society,* Bulletin No. 1 (1953), pp. 39–42.

A few important works provide a European vision of the Hasinai in the seventeenth and eighteenth centuries. One of the most useful is William Joyce Griffith, *The Hasinai Indians of East Texas as Seen by Europeans, 1687–1772,* Philological and Documentary Studies, 2 (New Orleans: Middle American Research Institute, Tulane University, 1954). Mattie Austin Hatcher edited and translated a number of Spanish documents, including reports from Fray Francisco Casanas de Jesús María, Fray Isidro Felís de Espinosa, and Fray Francisco Hidalgo, published as "Descriptions of the Tejas or Asinai Indians, 1691–1722," *Southwestern Historical Quarterly,* 30 (January 1927), pp. 206–218; ibid. (April 1927), pp. 283–304; ibid., 31 (July 1927), pp. 50–62; ibid. (October 1927), pp. 150–180. Herbert E. Bolton did extensive research on the Hasinai and the Spanish occupation while he was at the University of Texas. The results are included in *Texas in the Middle Eighteenth Century* (Berkeley: University of California Press, 1915); "The Native Tribes about the East Texas Missions," *Texas Historical Association Quarterly,* 11 (April 1908), pp. 249–276; and a manuscript on the Hasinai in the Bolton Collection at the University of California at Berkeley, which was published as *The Hasinais: Southern Caddoans as Seen by the Earliest Europeans,* ed. Russell M. Magnaghi (Norman: University of Oklahoma Press, 1987). These describe early Hasinai-Spanish relationships as they developed in the province of Texas. The Spanish documents provide a means of examining the bias of missionaries as they attempted to work with the Hasinai. They also describe the basic elements of society in hunting, agriculture, and government. There is little doubt that the Spanish considered the Hasinai confederacy the highest culture in the region between the Mississippi River valley and the Rio Grande valley. They also give insight into the Hasinai preference for the French over the Spanish, even into the present.

Elizabeth A. H. John's *Storms Brewed in Other Men's Worlds: The Confrontation of the Indians, Spanish, and French in the Southwest, 1540–1795* (College Station: Texas A&M University Press, 1975) provides a readable synthesis of the colonial period of struggle and confusion as the Hasinai attempted to deal with the Europeans. Odie B. Faulk's *The Last Years of Spanish Texas* (The Hague: Mouton, 1964) notes the peaceful relationships between the Hasinai and the Spanish, but chronicles the increasing difficulties when the United States purchased the Louisiana Territory from France. Late Spanish relationships with the Hasinai are the subject of Juan Antonio Padilla, "Texas in 1820," translated by Mattie Austin Hatcher, in *Southwestern Historical Quarterly,* 23 (1919), pp. 47–68. Other works that describe French activities during the eighteenth century include Fred B. Kniffen, Hiram F. Gregory, and George A. Stokes, *The Historic Indian Tribes of Louisiana, from 1542 to the Present* (Baton Rouge: Louisiana State University Press, 1987); William B. Glover, "A History of the Caddo Indians," *Louisiana Historical Quarterly* 18 (1935): 872–946; Ralph A. Smith, ed. and trans., "Account of the Journey of Benard de la Harpe," *Southwestern Historical Quarterly* 62 (1958–1959), pp. 75–86, 246–259, 371–385, 525–541; P. A. Kunkel, "The Indians of Louisiana about 1700," *Louisiana Historical Quarterly,* 34 (1951), pp. 175–204; and Richard Gaillard McWilliams, *Fleur de Lys and Calumet* (Baton Rouge: Louisiana State University Press, 1963). The networks of roads and trails were important to the trade of this and earlier periods, as evidenced in O. Lyon, "The Trail of the Caddo," *Arkansas Historical Quarterly,* 11 (1952): 124–130.

As the Mexican and Texas revolutions created chaos in the region, the position of the Hasinai and allied tribes deteriorated. A broad view of the entire northern border of Mexico touches on the Hasinai question in David J. Weber, *The Mexican Frontier, 1842–46* (Albuquerque: University of New Mexico Press, 1982). The French naturalist Jean Louis Berlandier left an interesting record in his *The Indian of Texas in 1830,* John C. Ewers, ed. (Washington: Smithsonian Institution, 1969), with illustrations of their dress at that time. An ethnohistorical approach to the same tribes is found in William W. Newcomb, *The Indians of Texas from Prehistoric to Modern Times* (Austin: University of Texas Press, 1969).

The Indian policy of the republic of Texas is described in several studies: Dorman H. Winfrey, ed., *Texas Indian Papers, 1825–1859* (3 vols., Austin: Pemberton Press, 1959) (includes not only correspondence concerning Sam Houston's treaty of 1837, the councils of 1843 that led to the Treaty of Bird's Fort, but also the United States treaty of 1846 and the removal of 1859); Ann Muckleroy, "The Indian Policy of the Republic of Texas," *Southwestern Historical Quarterly,* 25–26 (1922–1923); John H. Reagan, "The Expulsion of the Cherokee from East Texas," *Texas Historical Association Quarterly,* 1 (1897), and Walter Prescott Webb, "The Last Treaty of the Republic of Texas," *Southwestern Historical Quarterly,* 25 (1922).

This difficult period of transition in Texas is chronicled in several ways. Arrell M. Gibson's "An Indian Territory United Nations: The Creek Council of 1845," *Chronicles of Oklahoma,* 39 (Winter 1961–1962), pp. 398–413, notes the Caddo participation in concerted Indian efforts. The cultural efforts of Anglo-Americans vis-à-vis Texas Amerindians were interpreted in Murl L. Webb, "Religious and Educational Efforts among the Texas Indians in the 1850's," *Southwestern Historical Quarterly,* 69 (1966), pp. 22–37. The removal of the Hasinai and other tribes from Texas is recorded in Raymond Estep, ed., "Lieutenant William E. Burnet Letters: Removal of the Texas Indians and the Founding of Fort Cobb," *Chronicles of Oklahoma,* 38 (Autumn 1960), pp. 274–309; ibid. (Winter 1960–1961), pp. 369–396; ibid., 39 (Spring 1961), pp. 15–41, and Kenneth F. Neighbours, *Indian Exodus: Texas Indian Affairs, 1835–1859* (Quannah, 1973). Neighbours also wrote, "José María: Anadarko Chief," *Chronicles of Oklahoma,* 44 (Autumn 1966), pp. 254–274.

Very little has been published on the Hasinai in contemporary affairs. *The Ghost-Dance Religion and the Sioux Outbreak of 1890* by James Mooney (Chicago: University of Chicago Press, 1965) provides a sensitive account of Caddo participation in the ghost dance revival in Indian Territory. Vynola Beaver Newkumet and I wrote of postwar Hasinai leadership in "Melford Williams: Caddo Leadership Patterns in the Twentieth Century," *Journal of the West*, 23 (July 1984), pp. 64–69. The basis for governmental relations with the United States was published in *Constitution and By-Laws of the Caddo Indian Tribe of Oklahoma* (Washington: U.S. Government Printing Office, 1938); *Corporate Charter of the Caddo Indian Tribe of Oklahoma* (Washington: U.S. Government Printing Office, 1939); and *Constitution and By-Laws of the Caddo Indian Tribe of Oklahoma* in *Constitution and By-Laws* (Anadarko: Anadarko Area Office of the Bureau of Indian Affairs of the United States Government, c. 1985). The information collected in reference to the Indian Claims Commission efforts was published in Helen Hornbeck Tanner, *The Territory of the Caddo Tribe of Oklahoma* and *Commission Findings* (New York: Garland Publishing, Inc., 1974).

New expressions of Caddo visual artists and silversmiths are being recorded in contemporary art histories. The Caddo artist T. C. Cannon has been the subject of short studies, including *T. C. Cannon Memorial Exhibit* (New York: Aberbach Fine Art, 1979) and "T. C. Cannon, 1946–1978," by Edie Scott in *Southwest Art*, 11 (June 1981), pp. 76–79. In the modern arts, Silver Moon, Thompson Williams, and Cannon have found recognition for their work. Persons of all backgrounds can benefit from Hasinai forms in the search for self-expression.

INDEX